CHINESE VEGETARIAN COOKING

CHINESE VEGETARIAN COOKING

DEH-TA HSIUNG

HACKBERRY PRESS

A QUANTUM BOOK

Published by
Hackberry Press, a division of The Texas Bookman
2700 Lone Star Drive
Dallas
Texas 75212
USA

This edition printed 2003

ISBN 1-931040-22-2

QUMCCV-B

This book is produced by
Quantum Publishing Ltd
6 Blundell Street
London N7 9BH

Typeset in Great Britain by
Q.V. Typesetting Ltd., Eastbourne
Manufactured in Hong Kong by
Universal Color Scanning Ltd.
Printed in Singapore by
Star Standard Industries (Pte) Ltd.

CONTENTS

INTRODUCTION

Sweet and Sour Fish. A deep-fried 'fish' made with mashed taro (yam) and served with a sweet and sour sauce. (Green Cottage II).

Vegetarian cooking has a long history in China. Traditionally the Chinese have always been highly aware of, indeed one would almost say obsessed by, the link between food and health, whether physical or spiritual. Consequently many Chinese follow a vegetarian diet on health rather than economical grounds, although many are Buddhists who abhor the killing of any living creature and would certainly never dream of eating meat or fish in any form.

Until quite recently, many people believed that vegetarian cooking in China originated in the Buddhist temples, and that it was first introduced into China with Buddhism from India during the reign of the Han Emperor **Ming** (AD 58-75). Scholastic research carried out in China has now established that the earliest mention of vegetarianism on record was during the Zhou Dynasty (beginning **c.** 1028 BC); other references also exist in ancient texts all pre-dating the introduction of Buddhism into China by several hundred years. For example, in the earliest book on medicine written well over two thousand years ago entitled **Internal Channels**, the author advanced the 'five flavours' theory that one's body depends on five grains for nourishment, five fruits for support, five animals for benefit and five vegetables for charging-up!

It is generally agreed that the development of vegetarianism in China owed more to the introduction of many foreign fruits and vegetables during the Han Dynasty (206 BC-AD 222) than to Buddhism. Many Chinese vegetarians were influenced by the indigenous philosophy of Taoism, which developed the hygienic and nutritional science of food closely related to the basic **yin-yang** principles. The appearance of bean curd (tofu) — also during the Han Dynasty — and many other soy bean products, together with the discovery of making gluten from dough, helped to enrich and further diversify the vegetarian diet.

The close associations between Buddhists and the non-believer vegetarians are deep-rooted. One interesting point to note here is that despite their continual introduction, milk and dairy products are, to date, not prominent in Chinese cuisine. Therefore, unlike their counterparts in the West, Chinese vegetarians will not use butter, cheese or milk in their cooking, and a true Buddhist will eat neither eggs nor fish. Chinese vegetarians follow a nutritionally balanced diet based on pure vegetables, including fruits, nuts, mushrooms, fungus and cereal and bean products. All the essentials of a balanced diet are to be found in these vegetables: vitamins, protein, fats, carbohydrates and mineral salts. Naturally, the amount of these varies in different vegetables, but in no other type of food are they more readily assimilated.

The art of cooking vegetables has been perfected by the Chinese — the vegetables are almost always done lightly and simply. Obviously, different types of vegetables should be treated differently: a few require longer cooking time; others need to be cooked with more than one ingredient in order to gain the correct 'cross-blending' of flavours. All these are described in detail in the next section, and the 80 or so recipes are grouped under different methods of cooking rather than the ingredients used. Since this book is written for the average home cook in the Western world, I have included nothing which is so complicated and time-consuming that only a highly skilled professional chef could be expected to produce it.

ESSENTIAL TOOLS AND UTENSILS

The Chinese kitchen knife known as a cleaver appears to be hefty, gleaming and ominously sharp; in reality it is light, steady and not at all dangerous to use provided you handle it correctly and with care. I certainly regard it as one of the few essential tools for a Chinese kitchen. In the past I have noticed how my students completely changed their attitudes towards the cleaver once they tried using it for themselves. I think it depends on your state of mind, but once you have learnt to regard it as a cutting knife and not a chopper, you will surprise yourself as to how easy and simple it is to use.

The same thing can be said about using chopsticks. What appears to be hard work can be turned into great fun. I think the big mistake for most people who fail is that

they all too readily take the easy way out by reverting to a spoon and fork. What they do not seem to realize is that if you follow a few basic rules, you just cannot go wrong. My advice is this: first relax — you are not about to do something impossible. After all, if more than a quarter of the world's population can do it, why not you? The next thing to remember is not to concentrate too hard on your fingers and never mind the others — they are probably too busy themselves to be watching you!

In China, by far the most frequently used cooking method is quick stir-frying. The best result is obtained if you use a cooking utensil known as the wok.

The wok is cone shaped with a rounded bottom. The advantage of the wok is that because of its shape, the heat is evenly spread to all parts of the wok; therefore only a short cooking time is required. The ingredients naturally return to the centre of the wok however vigorously you stir them. The traditional wok is made of iron, and thus it retains a steady and intense heat.

A new wok should be seasoned before use. First, wash it in hot water and dry it by placing it over a moderate heat. Then wipe the inside with a pad of kitchen paper soaked in cooking oil until clean. After each use, wash it under hot or cold water. Never use any detergents, but scrape off any food that has stuck to the bottom with a hard brush or scourer. Dry the wok thoroughly over a moderate heat before putting it away, otherwise it will rust.

Besides stir-frying, the wok can also be used for deep-frying, shallow-frying, steaming, braising and boiling and so on. The type with a single handle is best suited for stir-frying; the two-handled type is better suited for all other purposes as it is more stable on top of a stove. The ordinary wok is not really suitable for an electric stove. If you do not cook with gas, then I suggest that you should get a wok with a flat bottom. Otherwise buy an electric wok; though not ideal, I have used it with fairly good results.

A Chinese bamboo steamer is another useful utensil to have in your kitchen. The advantage of the bamboo steamer over a conventional metal one is that the bamboo lid is not absolutely airtight, thus allowing a certain amount of evaporation which prevents condensation forming inside the lid.

BASIC TECHNIQUES AND COOKING METHODS

The main distinctive feature in Chinese cooking — vegetarian or otherwise — is the harmonious balance of colours, aromas, flavours and form, both in a single dish and a course of several different dishes.

Colour: Each ingredient has its own colour, and certain ingredients change their colour after cooking. You should bear this in mind when selecting different ingredients for blending of colour.

Aroma: Again each ingredient has its own aroma or fragrance, some pungent, some subtle. The Chinese like to use seasonings such as spring onions (scallions), ginger root and garlic in their cooking in order to enhance the various aromas in different ingredients. Another much used agent is rice wine, but if Chinese rice wine is unobtainable, a dry sherry is a good substitute.

Flavour: Flavour and taste are closely related to aromas and colours, and the principle of blending complementary flavours is a fundamental one — different ingredients must not be mixed indiscriminately. The matching of flavours should follow a set rather than a casual pattern.

Form: The preparation of ingredients is an important aspect of Chinese cooking: slices are matched with slices, shreds with shreds, cubes with cubes and so on. This is not just for the sake of appearance, which is of course another important element in Chinese culinary art, but also because ingredients of the same size and shape require about the same amount of time for cooking.

This complexity of interrelated elements of colour, aroma, flavour and form in Chinese cooking is reinforced by yet another feature: **texture**. A dish may have just one or several textures, such as tenderness, crispiness, crunchiness, smoothness and softness. The textures to be avoided are: sogginess, stringiness and hardness. The selection of different textures for a dish is another consideration when blending colours and flavours.

Before discussing the various cooking methods, I will first consider the importance of cutting techniques and

preliminary preparations.

To start with, when selecting the ingredients, always bear in mind the principle of harmonious balance of colour, aroma, flavours and textures. Some cooks like to mix contrasting flavours and unrelated textures; others prefer the matching of similar tastes and colours. Some wish the flavour of each ingredient to be preserved; others believe in the infusion of flavours. The blending of different flavours in a dish is itself a fine art, and in it lies the central principle of harmony.

Slicing: This is probably the most common form of cutting in Chinese cooking. The ingredients are cut into thin slices not much bigger than a large postage stamp.

Shredding: The ingredients are first cut into thin slices, then stacked up like a pack of playing cards and cut into thin strips about the size of matchsticks.

Dicing: The ingredients are first cut into coarse strips about the size of potato chips (French fries), then diced into cubes about the size of sugar cubes.

Diagonal cutting: This method is normally used for cutting vegetables such as carrots, celery, courgettes (zucchini) and asparagus. Roll the vegetable half a turn each time you make a diagonal cut straight down.

Mincing (grinding) or fine chopping: Finely chop the ingredients into small bits.

I mentioned the importance of texture in Chinese cooking earlier on. The desired texture or textures in any dish can only be achieved by the right cooking method. With the exception of quick stir-frying, which is distinctive to Chinese cooking, the various cooking methods used in China are basically very similar to those used in Western cooking: boiling, braising, deep-frying, shallow-frying, steaming and so on. The most important factors are that the vegetables should be young and tender — ideally they should be freshly picked but above all neither over cooked nor smothered with too much strong seasoning. Vegetables are seldom eaten raw in China, partly for hygiene reasons — both animal and human manures are widely used as fertilizers in the countryside. That is why you will find that most so-called Chinese salads are in fact pre-cooked and then served cold.

Boiling: Usually rapid boiling over a high heat. Thinly sliced or shredded ingredients are dropped into boiling stock or water to be cooked for one minute or less. Most soup dishes are cooked in this way.

Stir-frying: Thinly sliced or shredded ingredients are stir-fried in a little oil for a very short time. Timing here is of the utmost importance; overcooking will turn the food into a soggy mess. When correctly done, the food should be crispy and wholesome. Very little water or none at all is added, since the high heat will bring the natural juices out of the vegetables, particularly if they are fresh.

Braising: Normally a number of ingredients, some cooked, some semi-cooked, are blended together for the final stage of cooking in gravy.

Steaming: There are two methods of steaming. The first method is to place a plate or bowl containing the ingredients on the bottom rack of a steamer which is then put inside a wok containing boiling water; the steam passing through the steamer cooks the food. The second is to place the plate or bowl of ingredients on a wire or bamboo rack which fits half way down in a wok containing boiling water. Cover the wok so that the food is cooked by the rising steam inside the wok.

Deep-frying and shallow-frying: These are very similar to the basic methods normally used in the West.

REGIONAL COOKING STYLES

China is a vast country, with huge regional variations in climate and natural products. These differences are, naturally, reflected in the different cooking styles. Yet the fundamental character of Chinese cooking remains the same throughout the land: whether in the north (Peking cuisine) or in the south (Cantonese cooking), food is prepared and cooked in accordance with the same principle — most ingredients are cut up before cooking with great emphasis laid on heat control and the harmonious blending of different flavours. The chief distinguishing feature is that in the north, people rely more on wheat-flour as the basis of their diet, while in the south, it is almost always rice. Some of the cooking methods may vary a little from region to region; the emphasis on seasonings may differ too, but they are all unmistakably 'Chinese'.

Traditionally, the various styles of cooking are classified into four major groups according to their localities:

The Northern Group: represented by Peking and Shangdong with Henan and Shanxi sometimes included.

The Eastern Group: represented by Shanghai, Jiangsu, Zhejiang and Anhui (sometimes Hubei is included with this group).

The Western Group: represented by Sichuan and Hunan with Guizhou and Yunnan sometimes included.

The Southern Group: represented by Guangdong (Canton) and Fujian with Guangxi sometimes included. Because Canton was the first Chinese port opened for trade, foreign influences are particuarly strong in its cooking. Together with the neighbouring province of Fujian (Fukien), Canton is the place of origin of many Chinese emigrants overseas and Cantonese cooking not surprisingly the best known style of Chinese cooking abroad.

Monk's Travelling Companions. Deep-fried buns with vegetable stuffing served with a sweet and sour sauce dip. (Green Cottage II).

I have deliberately used the term 'group' rather than 'school' to differentiate the various regional cooking styles, for none of them can claim to form a distinct school of its own in the proper sense of the term. That unique distinction will have to be reserved for China's Buddhist School of cuisine.

Zhai, The Chinese word for vegetarianism, originally meant abstinence. Through the ages, the **Zhai** diet has developed into a speciality in the Chinese cuisine. The imagination and creativeness of skilled cooks in the Buddhist and Taoist temples have brought vegetarian

Cottage special. A mixture of different mushrooms, baby corns, fried gluten, carrots and mange-tout (snow) peas. (Green Cottage II).

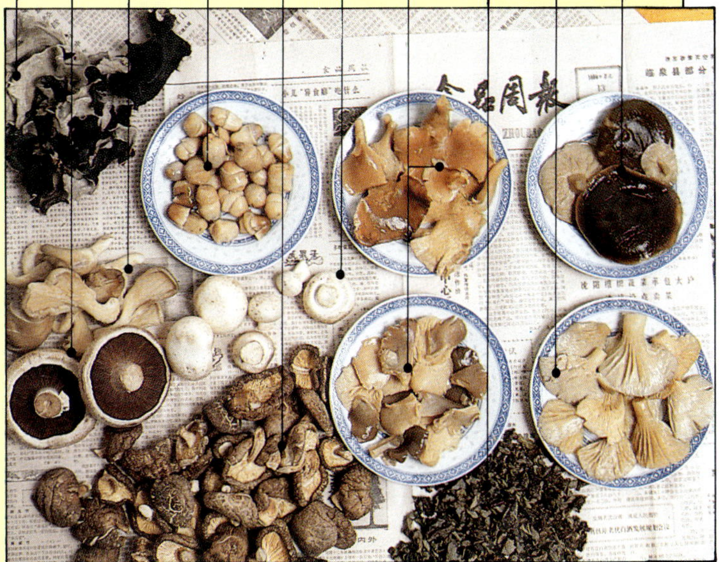

cooking to a level that rivals conventional Chinese cuisine. Prominent among the ingredients apart from fresh vegetables, are various edible fungi and mushrooms, bean curd (tofu) and different soy bean products, as well as gluten, known as imitation meats or vegetarian-meat, -chicken, or -fish and so on. Curiously these imitation meats bear an amazing resemblance to their fleshy counterparts in form, texture and flavours. The illustrations on this page were specially prepared for this book by the chefs from the newly opened **The Green Cottage II** in London, Europe's first Chinese vegetarian restaurant. Both Chef Lok and Chef Wong are from **Heung Chik Chiu**, the oldest established vegetarian restaurant in Hong Kong.

All these elaborate preparations of imitation meats are beyond the skills of ordinary Chinese housewives and home cooks. The very idea of them is contrary to the principle of vegetarianism, advocated originally on the grounds that natural, wholesome food could be obtained simply and economically for the people.

One of the best known poets from the Southern Song period, Lu You (AD 1125-1210) was a noted vegetarian. He suspected the carnivorous habit of being the cause of many diseases and regarded vegetarianism as the only healthy diet. Since he lived to a ripe old age of 86 (this was in the days when the average life expectancy in China was probably way below that of 50), he may well have been right. Indeed, recent medical research has produced conclusive evidence that the Chinese vegetarian diet contains some of the most powerful natural cancer-fighting substances.

SPECIAL INGREDIENTS AND SEASONINGS

A Chinese cook can always produce a Chinese meal wherever he or she may be without using any special ingredients. However, there are certain items which are commonly available outside China which will add just that exotic touch to your everyday cooking.

Bamboo shoots: Available in cans only. Once opened, the contents may be kept in water in a covered container for up to a week in the refrigerator. Try to find **Winter Bamboo-shoots** which are extra tender and delicious.

Bean curd (Tofu): This custard-like preparation of blended and pressed soy beans is exceptionally high in protein. It is sold in 7.5 cm (3 in) square cakes about 2.5 cm (1 in) thick in Oriental and health food stores. It will keep for a

SPECIAL INGREDIENTS AND SEASONINGS

Dried noodles

Fresh noodles

few days if submerged in water in a container and placed in a refrigerator.

Bean Sprouts: Fresh bean sprouts are widely available. They can be kept in the refrigerator for two to three days. Canned bean sprouts should not be used as they do not have the crunchy texture which is the main characteristic of this popular vegetable.

Bean thread (vermicelli): Made from mung beans, they are sold in dried bundles weighing from 50 g/2 oz to 450 g/1 lb. Soak in warm water for 5 minutes before use.

Black moss: Hair-fine, dark purple sea moss. Sold dried, it looks like black hair; used mostly in Buddhist and Chinese New Year festival dishes.

Chilli bean paste: Fermented bean paste mixed with salt, flour and hot chilli. It is sold in jars and can be substituted by mixing chilli sauce with crushed **yellow bean sauce.**

Chilli sauce: Hot, red sauce made from chillis, vinegar, sugar and salt. Use sparingly in cooking or as a dip sauce. Tabasco sauce can be substituted.

Chinese dried mushrooms: Widely used in many dishes as a complementary vegetable, both for their flavour and aroma. They must be soaked in warm water for 25-30 minutes (or in cold water for several hours) and then squeezed dry. The hard stalks should be discarded. Local dried mushrooms, though of slightly different flavour and fragrance, can be susbtituted.

Five-spice powder: A mixture of star anise, fennel seeds, cloves, cinnamon and Sichuan pepper. It is very strongly piquant, so it should be used sparingly. It will keep in a tightly covered container for many months.

Dried bean curd (tofu) skins

Uncooked and deep-fried bean curd (tofu)

Ginger root: Sold by weight, it should be peeled and sliced or finely chopped before use. It will keep for weeks in a dry, cool place. Ginger powder is no substitute.

Gluten: A high-gluten flour and water dough is soaked and kneaded in water to wash out the starch; the remaining gluten is porous like a sponge. It is cut into pieces to be used like dumplings to carry flavour and provide bulk in sauces.

Red bean paste: This reddish brown paste is made from blended red beans and crystal sugar. It is sold in cans which, once opened, should be transferred to a covered container and kept in the refrigerator (it keeps for several months). Sweetened blended chestnuts can be substituted.

Rice wine: Also known as **Shaoxing** wine, made from glutinous rice. **Saké** or pale dry or medium sherry can be substituted.

Salted black beans: Very salty indeed! Sold in plastic bags, jars or cans. Should be crushed with water or rice wine before use. They will keep indefinitely in a covered jar.

Sesame seed oil: Sold in bottles and widely used in China as a garnish rather than for cooking. The refined yellow sesame oil sold in Middle Eastern stores in not so aromatic, has less flavour and is therefore not a very satisfactory substitute.

Sichuan peppercorns: Also known as **hua chiao**, these reddish-brown peppercorns are much stronger and more fragrant than either black or white peppercorns. Sold in plastic bags, they will keep for a long time in a tightly sealed container.

SPECIAL INGREDIENTS AND SEASONINGS

Slender bamboo shoots

Sliced bamboo shoots

Braised bamboo shoots

Winter bamboo shoots

Pickled bamboo shoots

Bamboo shoots

SPECIAL INGREDIENTS AND SEASONINGS

Sichuan peppercorns

Star anise

Dried tangerine peel

Cinnamon

Five-spice powder

Mixed spices

Sichuan preserved vegetables: This is a speciality of Sichuan. It is the root of a special variety of green mustard pickled in salt and chilli. It is sold in cans, and once opened, should be stored in a tightly covered container; it will keep for months in the refrigerator.

Soy sauce: Sold in bottles or cans, this most popular Chinese sauce is used both for cooking and at the table. Whenever possible use **Light Soy Sauce** which has more flavour and does not discolour the food as much as the **Dark** or **Rich Soy Sauce**.

Sweet bean paste or Hoi Sin sauce: Made from soy bean sauce, sugar, flour, vinegar, salt, garlic, chilli and sesame seed oil. Will keep in the refrigerator for several months.

Tiger lily buds: Known as 'Yellow Flower' or 'Golden Needles' in Chinese, these are dried buds, golden yellow in colour. They have to be soaked and rinsed in water before use. Will keep indefinitely.

Water chestnuts: Available in cans only. Once opened, they will keep in fresh water for 2-3 weeks in a covered jar in the refrigerator.

White nuts: Also known as **gingko nuts**, they are the stones (or nuts) of the fruits from the gingko tree. Available canned, they are very popular with Chinese vegetarians.

Wood (tree) Ears: Also known as **Cloud ears**, these are dried black fungi. They should be soaked in water for 20 minutes and then rinsed in fresh water before use. They have a crunchy texture and a mild but subtle flavour.

Yellow bean sauce: This thick sauce is made from crushed yellow beans, flour and salt. It is sold in cans or jars; once opened, it should be transferred into a screw-top jar. It will keep in the refrigerator for months.

HOW TO PLAN YOUR MENU

As I have explained earlier, the four most important elements in Chinese cookery are colour, aroma, flavour and form. All these elements have to be well balanced to form a harmonious whole, both in a single dish and in a course of different dishes. Therefore it is quite logical that you should start your meal with light and delicate dishes and gradually work your way to rich and spicy dishes.

Another thing to remember is that the Chinese never serve an individual dish to each person, you all share all the dishes on the table. The only exception is for a light snack when a dish of **Chow mein** or a bowl of **Noodles in soup** is served — each person is given an individual portion.

HOW TO PLAN YOUR MENU

When planning the menu for a Chinese meal, the rule of thumb is to allow one dish for each person. Assuming you are cooking for a dinner party of six to eight people, you should start with two cold starters (or an assorted hors d'oeuvre), followed by two quick stir-fried dishes. Finally, serve rice with one or two long-cooked main courses together with a soup as an optional extra. This way you will not spend all your time in the kitchen.

The Chinese, with very few exceptions in certain parts of China, drink neither water nor tea during the meal, but soup instead. For those who prefer them, wine, beer or spirits are perfect partners for Chinese food.

Choosing wine to go with Chinese food should not present any problems. Red or white wine can be served with a Chinese meal according to personal taste.

China tea should be served without sugar or milk and only at the end of the meal — it is then most refreshing and invigorating.

Tea has been cultivated in China for well over 3,000 years and there is a very wide range of varieties which can be divided into five main groups: **Black, Green, Scented, Oolong** and **Brick**.

Black teas are prepared using the normal process of fermentation and they have a strong flavour and a honey-like aroma. The Chinese call them 'red' teas because of the colour of the brewed tea. The most famous black tea is Keemun Black.

Green teas are dried and roasted (like the black) but not fermented and they are consequently lighter and more subtly flavoured. The best known is *Longjing* (Dragon Well) produced in Hangzhou.

Oolong tea, which is only semi-fermented, is a special product of Fujian province and the most famous variety is *Tie Guanyin* (The Iron Goddess)

Ooling teas are particularly popular in south China and among expatriate Chinese in South East Asia.

Scented teas are prepared by adding dried flower petals such as jasmine, magnolia and rose petals to high quality green tea. These teas are more popular overseas than in China.

Brick teas are essentially black teas, fermented, roasted and dried but then compressed into oblong 'bricks'. They can be stored for a long time without losing their flavour.

True tea connoisseurs are very particular about the origin age, preparation and storage of their favourite brew. They also pay close attention to the quality and temperature of the water, and the kettle, the teapot and cups used in the brewing and serving. A good tea is judged by its colour, aroma and flavour and should be sipped and appreciated rather than just gulped down in a hurry.

COLD DISHES

There is an immense variety of cold dishes in Chinese cuisine. Some of them are served in small portions at the start of a meal as appetizers, while a number of other dishes are ideal for a buffet-style meal or as a part of the menu.

The big advantage of these dishes is that they can all be prepared and cooked long before being served. Their other advantage is that there is virtually no wastage, since any left-overs can be combined with other dishes, and served as assorted hors d'oeuvre.

Almost all of these dishes blend well with Western meals. Flexibility and diversity are two of the main aspects of Chinese cookery.

Tea eggs

SWEET AND SOUR CUCUMBER SALAD

1 cucumber
2 tsp finely chopped fresh ginger root
1 tsp sesame seed oil
2 tbsp sugar
2 tbsp rice vinegar

Preparation

1 Select a dark green and slender cucumber; the fat pale green ones contain too much water and have far less flavour. Cut it in half lengthwise, then cut each piece into slices. Marinate with the ginger and sesame seed oil for about 10-15 minutes.

2 Make the dressing with the sugar and vinegar in a bowl, stirring well to dissolve the sugar.

To serve

Place the cucumber slices on a plate. Just before serving, pour the sugar and vinegar dressing evenly over them and toss well.

HOT AND SOUR CUCUMBER — SICHUAN STYLE

1 cucumber
1 tsp salt
2 tbsp sugar
2 tbsp vinegar
1 tbsp chilli oil

Preparation

1 Split the cucumber in two lengthwise and then cut each piece into strips rather like potato chips (French fries). Sprinkle with the salt and leave for about 10 minutes to extract the bitter juices.

2 Remove each cucumber strip. Place it on a firm surface and soften it by gently tapping it with the blade of a cleaver or knife.

To serve

Place the cucumber strips on a plate. Sprinkle the sugar evenly over them and then add the vinegar and chilli oil just before serving.

CELERY SALAD

1 celery
1 tsp salt
7½ cups/1.7 l/3 pt water
2 tbsp light soy sauce
1 tbsp vinegar
1 tbsp sesame seed oil
2 slices fresh ginger root, finely shredded

Preparation

1 Remove the leaves and outer tough stalks of the celery. Thinly slice the tender parts diagonally. Blanch them in a pan of boiling, salted water. Then pour them into a colander and rinse in cold water until cool. Drain.

2 Mix together the soy sauce, vinegar and sesame seed oil. Add to the celery and toss well.

To serve

Garnish the salad with finely shredded ginger root and serve.

CHINESE CABBAGE SALAD

1 small Chinese cabbage
2 tbsp light soy sauce
1 tsp salt
1 tsp sugar
1 tbsp sesame seed oil

Preparation

1 Wash the cabbage thoroughly, cut into thick slices and place in a bowl.

2 Add the soy sauce, salt, sugar and sesame seed oil to the cabbage. Toss well and serve.

Note Green or red peppers (or both) can be added to the cabbage.

BEAN SPROUT SALAD

450 g / 1 lb fresh bean sprouts
1 tsp salt
10 cups / 2.3 l / 4 pt water
2 tbsp light soy sauce
1 tbsp vinegar
2 spring onions (scallions) finely shredded

Preparation

1 Wash and rinse the bean sprouts in cold water discarding the husks and other bits and pieces that float to the surface. It is not necessary to trim each sprout.

2 Blanch the sprouts in a pan of salted, boiling water. Pour them into a colander and rinse in cold water until cool. Drain.

3 Place the sprouts in a bowl or a deep dish and add the soy sauce, vinegar and sesame seed oil. Toss well and garnish with thinly shredded spring onions just before serving.

FRENCH (GREEN) BEAN AND RED PEPPER SALAD

225 g / 8 oz French (green) beans
1 medium or 2 small red peppers, cored and seeded
2 slices fresh ginger root, thinly shredded
1½ tsp salt
1 tsp sugar
1 tbsp sesame seed oil

Preparation

1 Wash the French beans, snip off the ends and cut into 5-cm / 2-in lengths. Cut the red peppers into thin shreds. Blanch them both in boiling water and drain.

2 Put the French beans, red peppers and ginger into a bowl. Add the salt, sugar and sesame seed oil. Toss well and serve.

TOMATO SALAD WITH SPRING ONION (SCALLION) AND OIL DRESSING

275 g / 10 oz hard (firm) tomatoes
1 tsp salt
1 tsp sugar
3-4 spring onions (scallions), finely chopped
3 tbsp salad oil

Preparation

1 Wash and dry the tomatoes. Cut them into thick slices. Sprinkle with salt and sugar. Leave to marinate for 10-15 minutes.

2 Place the finely chopped spring onions in a heat-resistant bowl. In a pan, heat the oil until quite hot and pour over the spring onions. Add the tomatoes, toss well and serve.

Note Other vegetables such as cucumber, celery and green peppers can be served in the same way.

SPICY CABBAGE — SICHUAN STYLE

450 g / 1 lb white cabbage
2 tsp salt
3-4 dried hot chilli peppers, soaked and finely chopped
3 spring onions (scallions), finely chopped
2 tsp fresh ginger root, finely chopped
2 tbsp sesame seed oil
2 tbsp sugar
50 ml / 2 fl oz water
2 tbsp vinegar

Preparation

1 Discard the outer tough leaves of the cabbage and cut the tender heart into thin slices. Sprinkle with salt and let stand for 3-4 hours. Pour off the excess water and dry the cabbage thoroughly. Place it in a bowl or a deep dish.

2 Heat the sesame seed oil in a pan until very hot. Add the finely chopped chillis, spring onions and ginger root. Stir for a few seconds and then add the sugar and water. Continue stirring to dissolve the sugar. Add the vinegar and bring the mixture to the boil. Remove the pan from the heat and allow the sauce to cool; then pour it over the cabbage. Cover the bowl or plate and leave to stand for 3-4 hours before serving.

PICKLED RADISHES

24 radishes
2 tsp sugar
1 tsp salt

Preparation

1 Choose fairly large radishes that are roughly equal in size, if possible, and cut off and discard the stalks and tails. Wash the radishes in cold water and dry them thoroughly. Using a sharp knife, make several cuts from the top about two-thirds of the way down the sides of each radish.

2 Put the radishes in a large jar. Add the sugar and salt. Cover the jar and shake well so that each radish is coated with the sugar and salt mixture. Leave to marinate for several hours or overnight.

3 Just before serving, pour off the liquid and spread out each radish like a fan. Serve them on a plate on their own or as a garnish with other cold dishes.

Pickled radishes

TEA EGGS

12 eggs
2 tsp salt
3 tbsp light soy sauce
2 tbsp dark soy sauce
1 tsp five-spice powder
1 tbsp red tea leaves

Preparation

1 Boil the eggs in water for 5-10 minutes. Remove and gently tap the shell of each egg with a spoon until it is cracked finely all over.

2 Place the eggs back in the pan and cover with fresh water. Add the salt, soy sauces, five-spice powder and tea leaves (the better the quality of the tea, the better the result). Bring to the boil and simmer for 30-40 minutes. Leave the eggs to cool in the liquid.

To serve

Peel off the shells — the eggs will have a beautiful marbled pattern. They can be served either on their own or as part of a mixed hors d'oeuvre, whole or cut into halves or quarters.

FIVE-SPICE BEAN CURD (TOFU)

4 cakes bean curd (tofu)
3 tbsp light soy sauce
2 tbsp dark soy sauce
1 tsp salt
1 tbsp white or brown sugar
3 tbsp rice wine or dry sherry
2-3 spring onions (scallions)
2-3 slices ginger root
2 tsp five-spice powder

Cooking

1 Place the bean curd in a saucepan and cover with cold water. Bring to the boil, cover and cook over a high heat for 10 minutes. By then the bean curd will resemble a beehive in texture.

2 Reduce the heat and add the soy sauces, salt, sugar, wine, spring onions, ginger root and five-spice powder. Bring to the boil gently under a cover and simmer for 30 minutes. Turn off the heat and leave to cool.

To serve

Remove the bean curd and cut it into small slices or strips. Serve them either on their own or as part of a mixed hors d'oeuvre.

PICKLED VEGETABLES

Use four to six of the following vegetables or more:

- cucumber
- carrot
- radish or turnip
- cauliflower
- broccoli
- green cabbage
- white cabbage
- celery
- onion
- fresh ginger root
- leek
- spring onion (scallion)
- red pepper
- green pepper
- string (green) beans
- garlic
- 5 qt / 4.5 l / 8 pt cold boiled water
- ¾ cup / 175 g / 6 oz salt
- 50 g / 2 oz chilli peppers
- 3 tsp / 15 g / ½ oz Sichuan peppercorns
- 50 ml / 2 fl oz Chinese distilled spirit (or white rum, gin or vodka)
- 100 g / 4 oz ginger root
- ½ cup / 100 g / 4 oz brown sugar

Preparation

1 Put the cold boiled water into a large, clean earthenware or glass jar. Add the salt, chillies, peppercorns, spirit, ginger and sugar.

2 Wash and trim the vegetables, peel if necessary and drain well. Put them into the jar and seal it making sure it is airtight. Place the jar in a cool place and leave the vegetables to pickle for at least five days before serving.

3 Use a pair of clean chopsticks or tongs to pick the vegetables out of the jar. Do not allow any grease to enter the jar. You can replenish the vegetables, adding a little salt each time. If any white scum appears on the surface of the brine, add a little sugar and spirit. The longer the pickling lasts, the better.

CRISPY 'SEAWEED'

You might be surprised or even shocked to learn that the very popular 'seaweed' served in Chinese restaurants is, in fact, green cabbage! Choose fresh, young spring greens with pointed heads. Even the deep green outer leaves are quite tender. This recipe also makes an ideal garnish for a number of dishes, particularly cold starters (appetizers) and buffet dishes.

- 750 g / 1½-1¾ lb spring (collard) greens
- 2½ cups / 575 ml / 1 pt oil for deep-frying
- 1 tsp salt
- 1 tsp sugar

Preparation

Wash and dry the spring green leaves and shred them with a sharp knife into the thinnest possible shavings. Spread them out on absorbent paper or put in a large colander to dry thoroughly.

Cooking

Heat the oil in a wok or deep-fryer. Before the oil gets too hot, turn off the heat for 30 seconds. Add the spring green shavings in several batches and turn the heat up to medium high. Stir with a pair of cooking chopsticks. When the shavings start to float to the surface, scoop them out gently with a slotted spoon and drain on absorbent paper to remove as much of the oil as possible. Sprinkle the salt and sugar evenly on top and mix gently. Serve cold.

Variation

Deep-fry 50 g / 2 oz split almonds until crisp and add to the 'seaweed' as a garnish, to give the dish a new dimension.

SOUPS

The Chinese do not have the habit of drinking water with their meals. Soups, most of them clear broths to which thinly sliced or shredded vegetables are added just before serving, have become almost a must at the Chinese table.

In the West, soups provide additional bulk to the meal and are always served at the start of the proceedings. In China, soups are meant either to act as a lubricant to help wash down the bulk and savoury foods, when served throughout the meal; on more formal occasions the soup or soups are served between courses to cleanse the palate.

A Chinese cook can make a nourishing and delicious soup merely by stir-frying a handful of fresh greens or whatever is to hand, with water and seasoning, and then bringing it to a rapid boil. Boiling water added to whatever is left from the main dish at the end of a meal also makes the perfect instant soup.

Bean sprout soup

TOMATO AND EGG FLOWER SOUP

250 g/9 oz tomatoes, skinned
1 egg
2 spring onions (scallions), finely chopped
1 tbsp oil
4 cups/1 l/1¾ pt water
2 tbsp light soy sauce
1 tsp cornflour (cornstarch) mixed with 2 tsp water

Preparation

1 Skin the tomatoes by dipping them in boiling water for a minute or so and then peel them. Cut into large slices.

2 Beat the egg. Finely chop the spring onions.

Cooking

Heat a wok or pan over a high heat. Add the oil and wait for it to smoke. Add the spring onions to flavour the oil and then pour in the water. Drop in the tomatoes and bring to a boil. Add the soy sauce and very slowly pour in the beaten egg. Add the cornflour and water mixture. Stir and serve.

CHINESE CABBAGE SOUP

250 g / 9 oz Chinese cabbage
3-4 dried Chinese mushrooms, soaked in warm water for 30 minutes
2 tbsp oil
2 tsp salt
1 tbsp rice wine or dry sherry
3¾ cups / 850 ml / 1½ pt water
1 tsp sesame seed oil

Preparation

Wash the cabbage and cut it into thin slices. Squeeze dry the soaked mushrooms. Discard the hard stalks and cut the mushrooms into small pieces. Reserve the water in which the mushrooms have been soaked for use later.

Cooking

Heat a wok or large pot until hot, add oil and wait for it to smoke. Add the cabbage and mushrooms. Stir a few times and then add the salt, wine, water and the mushrom soaking water. Bring to the boil, add the sesame seed oil and serve.

HOT AND SOUR SOUP

3 dried Chinese mushrooms, soaked in warm water for 30 minutes
2 cakes of bean curd (tofu)
50 g / 2 oz Sichuan preserved vegetables
50 g / 2 oz pickled vegetables, such as cucumber, cabbage or string (green) beans
2 spring onions (scallions), finely chopped
2 slices ginger root, thinly shredded
3¾ cups / 850 ml / 1½ pt water
1 tsp salt
2 tbsp rice wine or sherry
1 tbsp soy sauce
freshly ground pepper to taste
1 tsp sesame seed oil
1 tsp cornflour (cornstarch) with 2 tsp water

Preparation

1 Squeeze dry the mushrooms after soaking. Discard the hard stalks and cut mushrooms into thin shreds. Reserve the water for use later.

2 Thinly shred the bean curd. Sichuan preserved vegetables, pickled vegetables and ginger. Finely chop the spring onions.

Cooking

In a wok or large pot, bring the water to the boil. Add all the ingredients and seasonings and simmer for 2 minutes. Add the sesame seed oil and thicken the soup by stirring in the cornflour and water mixture. Serve hot!

Note A little vinegar can be added to the soup if you find that the pickled vegetables do not give a sour enough taste.

SPINACH AND BEAN CURD (TOFU) SOUP

225 g / 8 oz fresh spinach
2 cakes bean curd (tofu)
2 tbsp oil
2 tsp salt
2½ cups / 600 ml / 1 pt water
2 tbsp soy sauce
1 tsp sesame seed oil

Preparation

1 Wash the spinach well, discarding the tough and discoloured leaves. Shake off the excess water and cut the leaves into small pieces.

2 Cut the bean curd into about 14 pieces.

Cooking

1 In a wok or large pot, heat the oil until hot. Stir-fry the spinach until soft. Add the salt and water and bring to the boil.

2 Add the bean curd and soy sauce and cook for 1½-2 minutes. Add the sesame seed oil just before serving.

SWEETCORN (CORN) AND ASPARAGUS SOUP

- 175 g/6 oz white asparagus
- 1 egg white
- 1 tbsp cornflour (cornstarch)
- 2 tbsp water
- 2½ cups/500 ml/1 pt water
- 1 tsp salt
- 100 g/4 oz sweetcorn (corn kernels)
- 1 spring onion (scallion), finely chopped, to garnish

Preparation

1 Cut the asparagus spears into small cubes.

2 Beat the egg white lightly. Mix the cornflour with the water to make a smooth paste.

Cooking

1 Bring the water to a rolling boil. Add the salt, sweetcorn and asparagus. When the water starts to boil again, add the cornflour and water mixture, stirring constantly.

2 Add the egg white very slowly and stir. Serve hot, garnished with finely chopped spring onions.

Sweetcorn (corn) and asparagus soup *(opposite)*

BEAN SPROUT SOUP

- 225 g/8 oz fresh bean sprouts
- 1 small red pepper, cored and seeded
- 2 tbsp oil
- 2 tsp salt
- 2½ cups/600 ml/1 pt water
- 1 spring onion (scallion), finely chopped

Preparation

1 Wash the bean sprouts in cold water, discarding the husks and other bits and pieces that float to the surface. It is not necessary to top and tail (trim) each sprout.

2 Thinly shred the red pepper.

Cooking

1 Heat a wok or large pot, add the oil and wait for it to smoke. Add the bean sprouts and red pepper and stir a few times. Add the salt and water.

2 When the soup starts to boil, garnish with finely chopped spring onion and serve hot.

CHINESE MUSHROOM SOUP

6 dried Chinese mushrooms
2 tsp cornflour (cornstarch)
1 tbsp cold water
3 egg whites
2 tsp salt
2½ cups/600 ml/1 pt water
1 spring onion (scallion), finely chopped

Preparation

1 Soak the dried mushrooms in warm water for 25-30 minutes. Squeeze them dry, discard the hard stalks and cut each mushroom into thin slices. Reserve the water in which the mushrooms were soaked for use later.

2 Mix the cornflour with the water to make a smooth paste. Comb the egg whites with your fingers to loosen them.

Cooking

1 Mix the water and the mushroom soaking water in a pan and bring to the boil. Add the mushrooms and cook for about 1 minute. Now add the cornflour and water mixture, stir and add the salt.

2 Pour the egg whites very slowly into the soup, stirring constantly.

3 Garnish with the finely chopped spring onions and serve hot.

CUCUMBER SOUP

½ cucumber
50 g / 2 oz black field mushrooms
2½ cups / 600 ml / 1 pt water
1½ tsp salt
1 tsp sesame seed oil
1 spring onion (scallion), finely chopped

Preparation

1 Split the cucumber in half lengthwise, and thinly slice but do not peel.

2 Wash and slice the mushrooms, but do not peel.

Cooking

1 Bring the water to the boil in a wok or large pot. Add the cucumber and mushroom slices and salt. Boil for about 1 minute.

2 Add the sesame seed oil and finely chopped spring onion, stir and serve hot.

DEEP-FRIED BEAN CURD (TOFU) AND WOOD (TREE) EAR SOUP

- 50 g / 2 oz deep-fried been curd, or 1 cake fresh bean curd (tofu)
- 3-4 tbsp / 15 g / ½ oz wood (tree) ears (black fungus)
- 2½ cups / 600 ml / 1 pt water
- 1 tsp salt
- 1 tbsp light soy sauce
- 1 spring onion (scallion), finely chopped
- 1 tsp sesame seed oil

Preparation

1 Use either 2 packets of ready-made deep-fried bean curd (there are about 10 to each 25-g / 1-oz packet), or cut a cake of fresh bean curd into about 20 small cubes and deep-fry them in very hot vegetable oil until they are puffed up and golden. Cut them in half.

2 Soak the wood ears in water until soft (this will take about 20-25 minutes) and rinse until clean.

Cooking

1 Bring the water to the boil in a wok or large pot. Add the bean curd, wood ears and the salt.

2 When the soup starts to boil again, add the soy sauce and cook for about 1 minute. Garnish with finely chopped spring onion and sesame seed oil. Serve hot.

DRIED BEAN CURD (TOFU) SKIN AND VERMICELLI SOUP

15 g / ½ oz dried bean curd skin

⅔ cup / 25 g / 1 oz tiger lily buds

5 g / ¼ oz black moss

50 g / 2 oz bean thread vermicelli

3¾ cups / 850 ml / 1½ pt water

1 tsp salt

2 tbsp light soy sauce

1 tbsp rice wine or dry sherry

1 tsp finely chopped ginger root

2 spring onions (scallions), finely chopped

2 tsp sesame seed oil

fresh coriander to garnish

Preparation

1 Soak the bean curd skin in hot water for 30-35 minutes and then cut it into small pieces.

2 Soak the lily buds and black moss in water separately for about 20-25 minutes. Rinse the lily buds until clean. Loosen the black moss until it resembles human hair.

3 With a pair of scissors, cut the vermicelli into short lengths.

Cooking

1 Bring the water to the boil in a wok or large pot, and add all the ingredients together with the seasonings. Stir until well blended.

2 Cook the soup for 1-1½ minutes. Add the sesame seed oil and serve hot, garnished with coriander leaves.

QUICK STIR-FRIED DISHES

The Chinese cooking method of quick stir-frying is simple, economical, delicious and healthy.
All the ingredients are thinly sliced or shredded and then tossed and stirred in a little hot oil over high heat for a very short time. Most vegetables can be cooked in 1-1½ minutes. High heat and short cooking time help to preserve their natural flavours and textures. When correctly done, the vegetables should be crisp and bright; long, slow cooking over low heat will render the food into a soggy mess.
These quick stir-fried dishes are extremely attractive for the comparative newcomer to Chinese cooking because of the instant results. There is no need to spend hours in the kitchen bending over a hot stove; provided that you have selected the right ingredients, a simple but delicious meal of two or three stir-fried dishes for four to six people can be prepared, cooked and served in under an hour!

Stir-fried green and red peppers

STIR-FRIED BROCCOLI

250 g/9 oz broccoli
3 tbsp oil
1 tsp salt
1 tsp sugar
2 tbsp water

Preparation

Cut the broccoli into small pieces and remove the rough skin from the stalks.

Cooking

Heat the oil in a wok until hot and stir-fry the broccoli for about 1-1½ minutes. Add the salt, sugar and water and cook for a further 2 minutes. Serve hot.

Stir-fried broccoli

STIR-FRIED GREEN AND RED PEPPERS

1 large or 2 small green peppers, cored and seeded
1 large or 2 small red peppers, cored and seeded
3 tbsp oil
1 tsp salt
1 tsp sugar

Preparation

Cut the peppers into small diamond-shaped pieces; if you use one or two orange peppers, the dish will be even more colourful.

Cooking

Heat the oil in a hot wok or frying-pan until it smokes. Spread the oil with a scooper or spatula so that the cooking surface is well greased. Add the peppers and stir-fry until each piece is coated with oil. Add salt and sugar. Continue stirring for about 1 minute and serve if you like your vegetables crunchy and crisp. If not, you can cook them for another minute or so until the skin of the peppers becomes slightly wrinkled. Add a little water if necessary during the last stage of cooking.

STIR-FRIED LETTUCE

1 large cos (Romaine) lettuce

3 tbsp oil

1 tsp salt

1 tsp sugar

Preparation

Discard the tough outer leaves. Wash the remaining leaves well and shake off the excess water. Tear the larger leaves into 2 or 3 pieces.

Cooking

Heat the oil in a wok or large saucepan. Add the salt followed by the lettuce leaves and stir vigorously as though tossing a salad. Add the sugar and continue stirring. As soon as the leaves become slightly limp, transfer them to a serving dish and serve.

STIR-FRIED BEAN SPROUTS WITH GREEN PEPPERS

450 g / 1 lb fresh bean sprouts
1 small green pepper, cored and seeded
1-2 spring onions (scallions)
3 tbsp oil
1 tsp salt
1 tsp sugar

Preparation

1 Wash and rinse the bean sprouts in cold water, discarding the husks and other bits and pieces that float to the surface.

2 Cut the green pepper into thin shreds. Cut the spring onions into short lengths.

Cooking

1 Heat the oil in a hot wok until smoking. Add the spring onions and green pepper, stir a few times, and then add the bean sprouts. Continue stirring.

2 After about 30 seconds, add salt and sugar, and stir a few times more. Do not overcook because the sprouts will become soggy. This dish can be served either hot or cold.

STIR-FRIED ASPARAGUS

Choose the freshest asparagus available. The dark green and slender variety has more flavour than the pale, overgrown fat ones.

500 g / 1 lb asparagus
2 tbsp oil
1 tsp salt
1 tsp sugar

Preparation

Wash the asparagus well in cold water and discard the tough end of the stalk. Cut the tender part of the shoots into 2.5-cm / 1-in lengths, using the roll-cutting method: make a diagonal slice through the stalk, then roll it half a turn and slice again, so that you end up with diamond-shaped slices.

Cooking

Heat the oil in a very hot wok or frying-pan, swirling it to grease the pan well. Add the asparagus when the oil starts smoking. Stir-fry until each piece is coated with oil. Add salt and sugar and continue stirring for 1-1½ minutes only. No extra liquid should be added because it would spoil the colour and texture. This dish can be served either hot or cold.

STIR-FRIED COURGETTES (ZUCCHINI)

500 g / 1 lb courgettes (zucchini)
3 tbsp oil
2 tsp salt
1 tsp sugar
2 tbsp water

Preparation

Do not peel the courgettes; just trim off the ends. Split the courgettes in half lengthwise and cut each length diagonally into diamond-shaped chunks.

Cooking

Heat the oil in a wok. When the oil starts to smoke, put the courgettes in and stir-fry for about 30 seconds. Add the salt and sugar and cook for a further 1-1½ minutes, adding a little water if necessary. Serve hot.

STIR-FRIED GREEN PEPPERS, TOMATOES AND ONIONS

1 large or 2 small green peppers
1 large or 2 small hard (firm) tomatoes
1 large or 2 small onions
3 tbsp oil
1 tsp salt
1 tsp sugar

Preparation

Core and seed the green peppers and peel the onions. Cut all the vegetables into uniform slices.

Cooking

Heat the oil in a wok and wait for it to smoke. Add the onions and stir-fry for 30 seconds. Add the green peppers and continue cooking for 1 minute. Add the tomatoes, salt and sugar and cook for 1 minute more. Serve hot or cold.

THE 'TWO WINTERS'

The 'Two Winters' are winter bamboo shoots and winter mushrooms.

25 g / 1 oz dried Chinese mushrooms
225 g / 8 oz winter bamboo shoots
3 tbsp soy
2 tbsp oil sauce
1 tsp sugar
4 tbsp mushroom stock
1 tsp cornflour (cornstarch) mixed with 2 tsp water
1 tsp sesame seed oil

Preparation

1 Select mushrooms of uniform, small size. Soak them in warm water for about half an hour, squeeze dry and keep the water as mushroom stock.

2 Cut the bamboo shoots into thin slices not much bigger than the mushrooms.

Cooking

Heat the oil until it smokes. Stir-fry the mushrooms and bamboo shoots for about 1 minute. Add the soy sauce and sugar and stir a few more times. Add the mushroom stock, bring to the boil and cook for about 2 minutes. Add the cornflour and water mixture and blend well. Add the sesame oil and serve.

STIR-FRIED GREEN CABBAGE

Hot and sour cabbage — Shredded cabbage with red and green peppers — Stir-fried green cabbage

500 g / 1 lb green cabbage
3 tbsp oil
1½ tsp salt
1 tsp sugar

Preparation

Choose a small, fresh cabbage and discard any outer tough leaves. Wash it under the cold water tap before cutting it into small pieces. In order to preserve its vitamin content, cook it as soon as you have cut it to limit exposure to the air.

Cooking

Heat the oil in a hot wok until smoking, swirling it to cover most of the surface. Add the cabbage and stir-fry for about 1 minute. Add the salt and sugar and continue stirring for a further minute or so. Do not overcook because the cabbage will lose its crispness and its bright colour. No water is necessary since the high heat will bring out the natural juice from the cabbage, particularly if it is fresh. This dish can be served either hot or cold.

SHREDDED CABBAGE WITH RED AND GREEN PEPPERS

450 g / 1 lb white cabbage
1 green pepper
1 red pepper
3 tbsp oil
1 tsp salt
1 tsp sesame seed oil

Preparation

Thinly shred the cabbage. Core and seed the green and red peppers and thinly shred them.

Cooking

Heat the oil in a wok until hot. Add the cabbage and the peppers and stir-fry for 1-1½ minutes. Add the salt and stir a few more times. Add the sesame seed oil to garnish and serve either hot or cold.

EGGS WITH TOMATOES

250 g / 9 oz hard (firm) tomatoes

5 eggs

1½ tsp salt

2 spring onions (scallions), finely chopped

1 tsp finely chopped ginger root (optional)

4 tbsp oil

Preparation

1 Scald the tomatoes in a bowl of boiling water and peel off the skins. Cut each tomato in half lengthwise and then crosscut each half into wedges.

2 Beat the eggs with a pinch of salt and about a third of the finely chopped spring onions.

Cooking

1 Heat about half the oil in a hot wok or frying-pan and lightly scramble the eggs over a moderate heat until set. Remove the eggs from the wok.

2 Heat the wok again over high heat and add the remaining oil. When the oil is hot, add the rest of the finely chopped spring onions, the ginger root (if used) and the tomatoes. Stir a few times and then add the scrambled eggs with the remaining salt. Continue stirring for about 1 minute and serve hot.

Note Other vegetables such as cucumber, green peppers or green peas can be substituted for the tomatoes.

STIR-FRIED 'FOUR TREASURES'

Like Stir-fried mixed vegetables, the ingredients are specially selected to achieve a harmonious balance of colours, textures and flavours.

- 3-4 tbsp / 15 g / ½ oz wood (tree) ears (black fungus), dried
- 225 g / 8 oz broccoli
- 175 g / 6 oz bamboo shoots
- 100 g / 4 oz oyster mushroms
- 3-4 tbsp oil
- 1½ tsp salt
- 1 tsp sugar
- 1 tsp sesame seed oil

Preparation

1 Soak the wood ears in water for 15-20 minutes. Rinse until clean. Discard the hard roots if any and cut the extra large ones into smaller pieces.

2 Wash the broccoli and cut into whole florets. Do not discard the stalks; peel off the tough outer skin and cut them into small pieces.

3 Cut the bamboo shoots into slices, or, if using winter bamboo shoots, cut them into roughly the same size pieces as the broccoli stalks.

4 Wash and trim the mushrooms. Do not peel if using fresh ones. Canned oyster mushrooms are ready to cook; just drain off the water.

Cooking

1 Heat a wok or large frying-pan over high heat until really hot. Add the oil and wait for it to smoke. Then stir the oil with a scooper or spatula so that most of the surface of the wok is well greased.

2 Add the broccoli first, and stir until well coated with oil. Then add the bamboo shoots and mushrooms and continue stirring for about 1 minute. Add the wood ears, salt and sugar and stir for another minute or so. The vegetables should produce enough natural juices to form a thick gravy; if the contents in the wok are too dry, add a little water and bring to the boil before serving. The sesame seed oil should not be added until the very last minute.

AUBERGINE (EGGPLANT) WITH SICHUAN 'FISH SAUCE'

Sichuan 'fish sauce' is commonly served with fish but it does not have any fish in it.

- 450 g / 1 lb aubergines (eggplants)
- 4-5 dried red chilli peppers
- oil for deep frying
- 3-4 spring onions (scallions), finely chopped
- 1 slice ginger root, peeled and finely chopped
- 1 clove garlic, finely chopped
- 1 tsp sugar
- 1 tbsp soy sauce
- 1 tbsp vinegar
- 1 tbsp chilli bean paste
- 2 tsp cornflour (cornstarch), mixed with 2 tbsp water
- 1 tsp sesame seed oil

Preparation

1 Soak the dried red chillis for 5-10 minutes, cut them into small pieces and discard the stalks.

2 Peel the aubergines, discard the stalks and cut them into diamond-shaped chunks.

Cooking

1 Heat the oil in a wok and deep-fry the aubergines for 3½-4 minutes or until soft. Remove with a slotted spoon and drain.

2 Pour off the oil and return the aubergine to the wok with the red chillis, spring onions, ginger root and garlic. Stir a few times and add the sugar, soy sauce, vinegar and chilli bean paste. Continue stirring for about 1 minute. Finally add the cornflour and water mixture, blend well and garnish with the sesame seed oil. Serve either hot or cold.

BEAN CURD (TOFU) WITH MUSHROOMS

4 cakes bean curd (tofu)
3-4 medium-sized dried Chinese mushrooms
1 tbsp sherry
4 tbsp oil
1 tbsp soy sauce
1 tsp cornflour (cornstarch)
½ tsp salt
½ tsp sugar
1 tsp sesame seed oil

Preparation

1 Soak the dried mushrooms in warm water for about 30 minutes. Squeeze them dry and discard the stalks. Keep the water for use as stock.

2 Slice each square of bean curd into 6 mm-/ ¼ in-thick slices and then cut each slice into 6 or 8 pieces.

Cooking

Heat the oil in a wok and stir-fry the mushrooms for a short time. Add about ½ cup / 140 ml / ¼ pt of the water in which the mushrooms have been soaking. Bring to the boil and add the bean curd with the salt and sugar. Let it bubble for a while and then add the sherry and the sesame seed oil. Mix the cornflour with the soy sauce and a little water in a bowl and pour it over the bean curd in the wok so that it forms a clear, light glaze. Serve immediately.

STIR-FRIED CAULIFLOWER

1 cauliflower
3 tbsp oil
2 tsp salt
1 tsp sugar
4 tbsp water

Preparation

Wash the cauliflower in cold water and discard the tough outer leaves. Cut into florets with part of the stalk still attached.

Cooking

Heat the oil in a wok and stir-fry the cauliflower for about 1 minute. Add the salt, sugar and water and cook for a further 2 minutes or, if you prefer your vegetables well done, for 5 minutes, adding a little water if necessary. Serve hot.

STIR-FRIED CHINESE GREENS (RAPE)

This variety of Chinese cabbage has bright green leaves with pale green stems and sometimes a sprig of yellow flowers in the centre. Its other name is **rape**, and rape seed oil is widely used for cooking in China.

- 500 g / 1 lb Chinese green cabbage
- 1-2 slices ginger root, peeled
- 3 tbsp oil
- 1 tsp salt
- 1 tsp sugar
- 1 tbsp light soy sauce

Preparation

1 Wash the green cabbage and trim off any tough roots. Discard any outer, discoloured leaves.

2 Cut the peeled ginger root into small pieces.

Cooking

Heat the oil in a hot wok until it smokes and swirl it to cover most of the surface. Add the ginger root pieces to flavour the oil. Add the greens, stir for about 1 minute and then the salt and sugar. Continue stirring for another minute or so. Pour in the soy sauce and cook for a little longer. Serve hot. This dish is often used to add colour to a meal.

STIR-FRIED SPINACH AND BEAN CURD (TOFU)

- 225 g / 8 oz spinach
- 2 cakes bean curd (tofu)
- 4 tbsp oil
- 1 tsp salt
- 1 tsp sugar
- 1 tbsp soy sauce
- 1 tsp sesame seed oil

Preparation

Wash the spinach well, shaking off the excess water. Cut up each cake of bean curd into about 8 pieces.

Cooking

1 Heat the oil in a wok. Fry the bean curd pieces until they are golden, turning them over once or twice gently. Remove them with a slotted spoon and set aside.
2 Stir-fry the spinach in the remaining oil for about 30 seconds or until the leaves are limp. Add the bean curd pieces, salt, sugar and soy sauce, blend well and cook for another 1-1½ minutes. Add the sesame seed oil and serve hot.

STIR-FRIED GREEN BEANS AND BEAN SPROUTS

Dwarf French beans are best for this recipe. If they are not available, use thinly shredded runner beans or mange-tout.

- 225 g/8 oz green beans (haricots verts, runner beans or mange-tout (snow peas))
- 225 g/8 oz fresh bean sprouts
- 3-4 tbsp oil
- 1½ tsp salt
- 1 tsp sugar

Preparation

1 Wash and trim the beans. Shred if necessary.

2 Wash and rinse the bean sprouts in a bowl of cold water and discard the husks and other bits and pieces that float to the surface.

Cooking

1 Heat the oil in a hot wok or large frying-pan and when it starts to smoke, swirl the wok so that its surface is well greased. Add the green beans first, stirring to make sure that each piece is well covered with oil, then the bean sprouts and stir-fry for about 30 seconds. Add the salt and the sugar.

2 Continue stirring for about 1 minute at the most. Overcooking will turn both the green beans and bean sprouts into a soggy mass.

STIR-FRIED FRENCH (GREEN) BEANS WITH BABY CORN

If fresh baby corn (also known as dwarf or young corn) is not available, use canned. You will need about 350-400 g/12-14 oz drained weight of corn.

225 g/8 oz French (green) beans
225 g/8 oz baby corn
3-4 tbsp oil
1½ tsp salt
1 tsp sugar
2 tbsp water

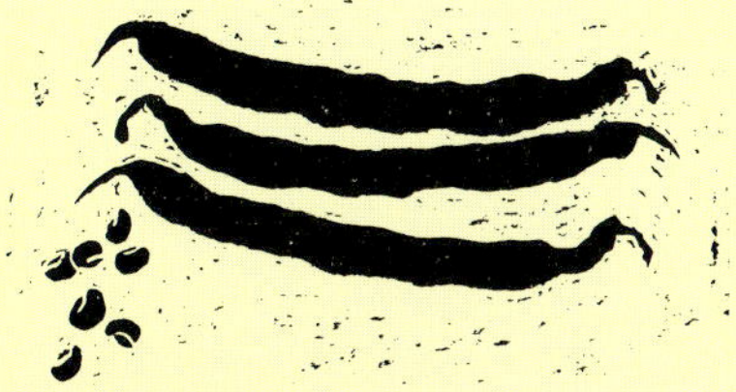

Preparation

1 Wash and trim the beans.

2 Depending on the size of the baby corns, leave them whole if small, or cut them into two or three diamond-shaped pieces if larger.

Cooking

1 Heat a wok or large frying-pan over a high heat until very hot, add the oil and swirl it so that the cooking surface is well greased. When the oil starts to smoke, add the French beans and baby corn and stir-fry for about 1 minute. Add the salt and sugar and continue stirring for another minute or so. Add the water if the vegetables dry out before they are cooked.

2 Serve as soon as all the liquid has evaporated. If you prefer your vegetables slightly underdone, serve when there is still a little juice left in the wok.

STIR-FRIED MANGE-TOUT (SNOW PEAS) WITH CHINESE MUSHROOMS

6-8 dried Chinese mushrooms
225 g/8 oz mange-tout (snow peas)
3 tbsp oil
1 tsp salt
1 tsp sugar

Preparation

1 Soak the dried mushrooms in warm water for 25-30 minutes. Squeeze dry and discard the hard stalks. Keep the water. Cut each mushroom into small pieces.

2 Wash and trim the mange-tout peas. If large, they should be snapped in half. Smaller ones can be left whole.

Cooking

Heat the oil in a very hot wok or large frying-pan until smoking. Cook the mange-tout peas by stir-frying for a few seconds. Then add the mushrooms, the salt and sugar and continue stirring for about 30 seconds. Add a little of the water in which the mushrooms were soaked. Serve as soon as the liquid starts to boil.

Note A little cornflour (cornstarch) mixed with cold water can be added to thicken the liquid at the last minute.

STIR-FRIED MIXED VEGETABLES

- 100 g/4 oz Chinese cabbage
- 100 g/4 oz carrots
- 100 g/4 oz mange-tout (snow peas)
- 5-6 dried Chinese mushrooms
- 3 tbsp oil
- 1 tsp salt
- 1 tsp sugar
- 1 tsp water

Preparation

Soak the dried mushrooms in warm water for 25-30 minutes. Squeeze them dry, discard the hard stalks and cut into thin slices. Trim the mange-tout peas and cut the Chinese cabbage and carrots into slices.

Cooking

Heat the oil in a preheated wok. Add the Chinese cabbage, carrots, mange-tout peas and dried mushroom and stir-fry for about 1 minute. Add the salt and sugar and stir for another minute or so with a little more water if necessary. Do not overcook or the vegetables will lose their crunchiness. Serve hot.

STIR-FRIED CELERY WITH MUSHROOMS

1 small head of celery
100 g/4 oz white mushrooms
3 tbsp oil
1½ tsp salt
1 tsp sugar

Preparation

1 Wash the celery and thinly slice the stalks diagonally.

2 Wash the mushrooms and cut them into thin slices. Do not peel.

Cooking

1 Heat the oil in a hot wok or frying-pan until it smokes, swirling it so that it covers most of the surface.

2 Add the celery and mushrooms and stir-fry for about 1 minute or until each piece is coated with oil. Add the salt and sugar and continue stirring. Add a little water if the contents get too dry. Do not overcook because the celery will lose its crunchy texture. This dish can be served either hot or cold.

STIR-FRIED LEEKS WITH WOOD (TREE) EARS

3-4 tbsp / 15 g / ½ oz wood (tree) ears (black fungus)
450 g / 1 lb leeks
3 tbsp oil
1 tsp salt
1 tsp sugar
1 tsp sesame seed oil

Preparation

1 Soak the wood ears in water for 20-25 minutes, rinse well and discard the hard roots if any. Drain.

2 Wash the leeks and cut them diagonally into chunks.

Cooking

Heat the oil in a hot wok or frying-pan. Use your scooper or spatula to spread the oil so that most of the surface is well greased. When the oil starts to smoke, add the leeks and wood ears, and stir-fry for about 1 minute. Add the salt and sugar and continue stirring. Wet with a little water if necessary. Add the sesame seed oil to garnish and serve hot.

FRIED 'POCKETED EGGS'

Eggs are frequently cooked this way in China. The only preparation you will need to do is to chop the spring onion (scallion) very finely.

4 eggs
2-3 tbsp oil
1 tbsp light soy sauce
1 spring onion (scallion), finely chopped

Cooking

Heat the oil in a hot wok or frying-pan and fry the eggs on both sides. Add the soy sauce and a little water and braise for 1-2 minutes. Garnish with spring onion and serve hot.

Taking a bite of the egg and finding the yolk inside the white is rather like finding something in a pocket — hence the name of this dish.

HOT AND SOUR CABBAGE

700 g / 1½ lb white cabbage
10 Sichuan peppercorns
5 small dried red chilli peppers
3 tbsp oil
2 tbsp soy sauce
1½ tbsp vinegar
1½ tbsp sugar
1½ tsp salt
1 tsp sesame seed oil

Preparation

Choose a round, pale green cabbage with a firm heart — never use loose leafed cabbage. Wash in cold water and cut the leaves into small pieces the size of a matchbox. Cut the chillis into small bits. Mix the soy sauce, vinegar, sugar and salt to make the sauce.

Cooking

Heat the oil in a preheated wok until it starts to smoke. Add the pepercorns and the red chillis and a few seconds later the cabbage. Stir for about 1½ minutes until it starts to go limp. Pour in the prepared sauce and continue stirring for a short while to allow the sauce to blend in. Add the sesame seed oil just before serving. This dish is delicious both hot and cold.

VEGETARIAN CHOP SUEY

Many of you know that **chop suey** is a creation of the West, but we do have in China a dish called **tsa-sui**, which literally means 'miscellaneous fragments', or 'mixed bits and pieces'. The genuine article should have all the ingredients specially selected in order to achieve the desired harmonious balance of colours, textures and flavours. It should never be the soggy mass one often finds in a cheap take-away.

- 2 cakes of bean curd (tofu)
- 2 tbsp / 10 g / ¼ oz wood (tree) ears (black fungus), dried
- 175 g / 6 oz broccoli or mange-tout (snow peas)
- 175 g / 6 oz bamboo shoots
- 100 g / 4 oz mushrooms
- 4-5 tbsp oil
- 1½ tsp salt
- 1 tsp sugar
- 1-2 spring onions (scallions), finely chopped
- 1 tbsp light soy sauce
- 2 tbsp rice wine or dry sherry
- 1 tsp cornflour (cornstarch) mixed with 1 tbsp cold water

Preparation

1 Cut the bean curd into about 24 small pieces. Soak the wood ears in water for about 20-25 minutes, rinse them clean and discard any hard roots.

2 Cut the broccoli and bamboo shoots into uniformly small pieces.

Cooking

1 Heat a wok over a high heat, add about half of the oil and wait for it to smoke. Swirl the pan so that its surface is well greased. Add the bean curd pieces and shallow-fry them on both sides until golden, then scoop them out with a slotted spoon and set them aside.

2 Heat the remaining oil and add the broccoli. Stir for about 30 seconds and then add the wood ears, bamboo shoots and the partly cooked bean curd. Continue stirring for 1 minute and then add the salt, sugar, spring onions, soy sauce and wine. Blend well and when the gravy starts to boil, thicken it with the cornflour and water mixture. Serve hot.

BRAISED & STEAMED DISHES

The dishes which constitute the main courses in the serving sequence of a conventional Chinese meal take a little longer to cook. They can be prepared and cooked well in advance, so avoiding a last minute rush. Some of these dishes can be served cold and are ideal buffet food. Again, most of them blend well with Western food, and almost all of these can be served either on their own as a complete meal, or in conjunction with non-Chinese food as part of a menu.

Chinese cabbage casserole

CHINESE CABBAGE CASSEROLE

- 450 g/1 lb Chinese cabbage
- 50 g/2 oz deep-fried bean curd or 2 cakes fresh bean curd (tofu)
- 100 g/4 oz carrots
- 3 tbsp oil
- 1 tsp salt
- 1 tsp sugar
- 2 tbsp light soy sauce
- 2 tbsp rice wine or dry sherry
- 1 tsp sesame seed oil

Preparation

1 Separate the Chinese cabbage leaves, wash and cut them into small pieces. If using fresh bean curd, cut each cake into about 12 pieces and fry them in a little oil until golden.

2 Peel the carrots and cut them into diamond-shaped chunks.

Cooking

1 Heat the oil in a hot wok and stir-fry the cabbage with the salt and sugar for a minute or so. Transfer it to a Chinese sand-pot or casserole and cover it with the bean curd, carrots, soy sauce and sherry. Put a lid on the pot and when it comes to the boil reduce the heat and simmer for 15 minutes.

2 Stir in the sesame oil. Add a little water if necessary and cook for a few more minutes. Serve hot.

BRAISED CHINESE BROCCOLI

450 g / 1 lb Chinese broccoli
3 tbsp oil
1 tsp salt
1 tsp sugar
1 tbsp soy sauce

Preparation

Trim off the tough leaves and blanch the rest in slightly salted boiling water until soft. Remove and strain.

Cooking

Heat a wok until hot. Add the oil and wait until it starts to smoke. Stir-fry the broccoli with the salt and sugar for 1½-2 minutes. Remove and arrange neatly on a long serving dish. Pour on the soy sauce and serve.

CHINESE CABBAGE AND MUSHROOMS

6-8 dried Chinese mushrooms
450 g / 1 lb Chinese cabbage leaves
3 tbsp oil
1 tsp salt
1 tsp sugar
1 tbsp soy sauce
1 tsp sesame seed oil

Preparation

Soak the mushrooms in warm water for about 20 minutes. Squeeze them dry and discard the hard stalks. Keep the water. Cut each mushroom in half or into quarters depending on the size. Cut the cabbage leaves into pieces about the size of a large postage stamp.

Cooking

Heat the oil in a wok, add the cabbage and the mushrooms and stir-fry until soft. Add the salt, sugar and soy sauce and cook for a further 1½ minutes. Mix in some of the water in which the mushrooms were cooked and the sesame seed oil.

BRAISED BRUSSELS SPROUTS

500 g / 1 lb Brussels sprouts
4 tbsp oil
2 tsp salt
1 tsp sugar
3 tbsp water

Preparation

Wash the Brussels sprouts and discard all the tough outer leaves. Trim the roots and make a cross-cut at the base.

Cooking

Heat a wok until hot, add the oil and wait for it to smoke. Swirl the wok so that it is well oiled, add the sprouts and stir for 1-1½ minutes. When all the sprouts are well covered with oil, add the salt and sugar and continue stirring. Add the water to the wok, braise for about 1 minute, and then stir a few more times. Add more liquid if necessary. Small sprouts require 2-3 minutes to cook through; larger ones may take a minute or so longer. Serve hot.

CHINESE CABBAGE AND STRAW MUSHROOMS IN CREAM SAUCE

400 g / 14 oz Chinese cabbage
350 g / 12 oz canned straw mushrooms or 225 g / 8 oz fresh straw mushrooms
4 tbsp oil
1½ tsp salt
1 tsp sugar
1 tbsp cornflour (cornstarch) mixed with 3 tbsp cold water
125 ml / 4 fl oz milk

Preparation

1 Separate the cabbage leaves and cut each leaf in half lengthwise.

2 Drain the straw mushrooms. If using fresh ones, do not peel them but just wash and trim off the roots.

Cooking

1 Heat 3 tbsp oil in a hot wok and stir-fry the cabbage leaves for about 1 minute. Add the salt and sugar and continue stirring for another minute or so. Remove the cabbage leaves and arrange them neatly on one side of a serving dish.

2 Heat the remaining oil until hot, then reduce the heat and add the cornflour and water mixture and the milk and stir until thickened. Pour about half of the sauce into a jug (pitcher) and keep warm.

3 Add the mushrooms to the remaining sauce in the wok and heat them thoroughly over high heat. Remove the mushrooms and place them next to the cabbage leaves on the plate. Pour the sauce from the jug evenly over the cabbage and mushrooms and serve hot.

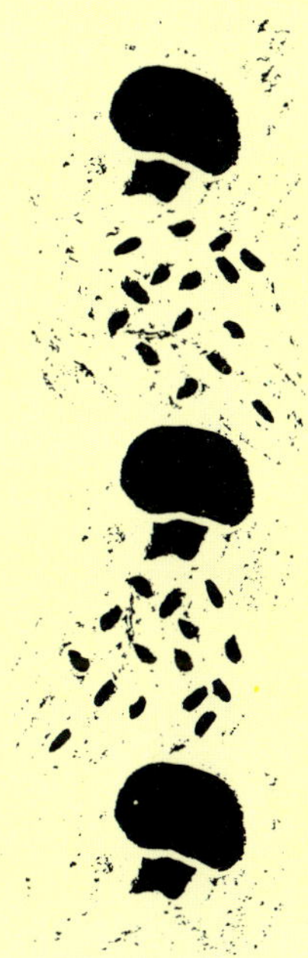

STEAMED CAULIFLOWER

1 medium-sized cauliflower
1 tsp salt
1 tbsp rice wine or dry sherry
1 tbsp sesame seed oil
1 cube fermented red bean curd

Preparation

When choosing cauliflower, make sure the leaves that curl round the flower are bright green and not withered. Bright leaves show that the cauliflower is fresh. Wash the cauliflower well under the cold water tap, trim off the hard root and discard the tough outer leaves. Keep a few of the tender leaves on as they add to the colour and flavour.

Cooking

1 Place the cauliflower in a snugly fitting bowl. Mix salt, wine and sesame seed oil and pour them evenly over the cauliflower, covering its entire surface. Place the bowl in a steamer and cook over high heat for 10-15 minutes.

2 To serve, remove bowl from the steamer. Crush the fermented red bean curd with a little sauce and pour it over the cauliflower. You should be able to break the cauliflower into florets either with a spoon or a pair of chopsticks. Serve hot.

STEAMED EGGS

5 eggs
4 tbsp hot water
1 tsp salt
2 tsp rice wine
1 tbsp soy sauce
Spinach leaves, chopped (optional)

Preparation

Beat the eggs in a bowl, and mix in the water, salt and rice wine.

Cooking

Place the bowl, uncovered, in a saucepan half-filled with boiling water. Cover the saucepan and steam gently for 20 minutes. If the heat is too high, the eggs will not congeal, or holes will form. A garnish of chopped spinach leaves may be added before steaming. Add the soy sauce before serving.

'BUDDHA'S DELIGHT'—EIGHT TREASURES OF CHINESE VEGETABLES

The original recipe calls for eighteen different ingredients to represent the eighteen Buddhas. Later this was reduced to eight, usually consisting half of dried and half of fresh vegetables.

15 g / ½ oz dried bean curd (tofu) skin sticks
⅓ cup / 15 g / ½ oz dried tiger lily buds
3-4 tbsp / 15 g / ½ oz dried wood (tree) ears (black fungus)
10 g / ¼ oz dried black moss (hair)
50 g / 2 oz bamboo shoots
50 g / 2 oz lotus root
50 g / 2 oz straw mushrooms
50 g / 2 oz white nuts
4 tbsp oil
1½ tsp salt
1 tsp sugar
1 tbsp light soy sauce
1 tsp cornflour (cornstarch) mixed with 1 tbsp cold water
2 tsp sesame seed oil

Preparation

1 Soak the dried vegetables separately in cold water overnight or in warm water for at least 1 hour. Cut the bean curd sticks into short lengths.

2 Cut the bamboo shoots and lotus root into small slices. The straw mushrooms and white nuts can be left whole.

Cooking

1 Heat a wok or large frying-pan. When it is hot, put in about half of the oil and wait until it smokes. Stir-fry all the dried vegetables together with a little salt for about 1 minute. Remove and set aside.

2 Add and heat the remaining oil and stir-fry the rest of the vegetables and the salt for about 1 minute. Add the partly cooked dried vegetables, the sugar and soy sauce stirring constantly. If the contents start to dry out, pour in a little water. When the vegetables are cooked, add the cornflour and water mixture to thicken the gravy. Garnish with the sesame seed oil just before serving. This dish can be served either hot or cold.

BRAISED BAMBOO SHOOTS

450 g / 1 lb slender bamboo shoots
3 tbsp oil
2 tbsp rice wine or dry sherry
1 tbsp sugar
2 tbsp light soy sauce
1 tbsp dark soy sauce
2 tsp sesame seed oil

Preparation

If possible, use the 'Evergreen' brand slender bamboo shoots, a speciality from Kiangsi province in south-east China; they need only be drained and they are ready to cook. The next best are 'Maling' bamboo shoots from Shanghai. If you can get winter bamboo shoots, so much the better. Drain off the water and slice each shoot lengthwise into thin strips.

Cooking

Heat the oil in a hot wok or frying-pan, add the bamboo shoots and stir-fry until well covered with oil. Add the wine, sugar and both soy sauces and continue stirring. Braise for about 3-4 minutes or until almost all the liquid has evaporated. Add the sesame seed oil and serve either hot or cold.

FRIED GLUTEN

Mianjin in Chinese, gluten is also known as mock meat or chicken in Chinese cuisine. It is made by kneading a flour and water dough in water to wash out much of the starch. The remaining gluten is porous like a sponge; cut into pieces it can be used like dumplings to hold flavour and to give substance to a liquid sauce.

8 cups / 1 kg / 2 lb flour
1 tbsp salt
500-550 ml / 18-19 fl oz warm water
oil for deep-frying
1 tsp salt
1 tsp sugar
1 tbsp light soy sauce
¼ tsp monosodium glutamate (optional)

Preparation

1 Sift the flour into a large mixing bowl. Add the salt and the water gradually to make a firm dough. Knead until smooth and then cover with a damp cloth and leave to stand for about 1 hour.

2 Place the dough in a large colander or sieve and run cold water over it while you press and squeeze the dough with your hands to wash out as much of the starch as you can. After 10-15 minutes of this hard work, you will end up with about 300 g / 11 oz gluten. Squeeze off as much water as you can and then cut the gluten into about 35-40 small pieces. These can be cooked either by deep-frying or boiling (or they can be steamed or baked).

Cooking

1 Heat the oil in a wok or deep-fryer. When hot, deep-fry the gluten in batches — about 6 to 8 at a time — for about 3 minutes or until they turn golden. Remove and drain.

2 Pour off the excess oil leaving about 1 tablespoon in the wok. Return the partly cooked gluten to the wok, add salt, sugar and soy sauce (and the monosodium glutamate if used), stir, and add a little water if necessary. Braise for about 2 minutes. Serve hot or cold.

KAO FU — STEWED GLUTEN IN SWEET BEAN SAUCE

See the recipe for Fried Gluten (page 95).

300 g/11 oz gluten in small pieces
3 tbsp oil
1 tbsp dark soy sauce
1 tbsp sugar
1 tsp five-spice powder
2 tbsp rice wine or dry sherry
1 tbsp sweet bean paste or **hoi sin** sauce
1 slice ginger root, peeled
2 tsp sesame seed oil

Preparation

Boil the gluten pieces in a pan of water for about 4-5 minutes or until they float to the surface. Remove and drain off as much water as possible.

Cooking

1 Heat the oil in a hot wok or pan. When hot, add the boiled gluten, stir for a few seconds and then add the soy sauce, sugar, five-spice powder, wine, sweet bean paste, crushed ginger root and about 125 ml/4 fl oz water. Bring to the boil and cook over high heat for 20-25 minutes or until there is very little juice left, stirring now and again to make sure that each piece of gluten is well covered by the gravy.

2 Add the sesame seed oil, blend well and serve hot or cold.

CASSEROLE OF VEGETABLES

2 tbsp / 10 g / ¼ oz dried wood (tree) ears (black fungus)

1 cake bean curd (tofu)

100 g / 4 oz French (green) beans or mange-tout (snow peas)

100 g / 4 oz cabbage or broccoli

100 g / 4 oz baby corn or bamboo shoots

100 g / 4 oz carrots

3-4 tbsp oil

1 tsp salt

1 tsp sugar

1 tbsp light soy sauce

1 tsp cornflour (cornstarch) mixed with 1 tbsp cold water

Preparation

1 Soak the wood ears in water for 20-25 minutes, rinse them and discard the hard roots, if any.

2 Cut the bean curd into about 12 small pieces and harden the pieces in a pot of lightly salted boiling water for 2-3 minutes. Remove and drain.

3 Trim the French beans or mange-toute peas. Leave whole if small; cut in half if large.

4 Cut the vegetables into thin slices or chunks.

Cooking

1 Heat about half of the oil in a flameproof casserole or saucepan. When hot, lightly brown the bean curd on both sides. Remove with a slotted spoon and set aside.

2 Heat the remaining oil and stir-fry the rest of the vegetables for about 1½ minutes. Add the bean curd pieces, salt, sugar and soy sauce and continue stirring to blend everything well. Cover, reduce the heat and simmer for 2-3 minutes.

3 Mix the cornflour with water to make a smooth paste, pour it over the vegetables and stir. Increase the heat to high just long enough to thicken the gravy. Serve hot.

FU-YUNG BEAN CURD (TOFU)

In most Chinese restaurants, **fu yung** means 'omelette', but strictly speaking, it should mean scrambled egg whites with a creamy texture.

1 cake bean curd (tofu)

4 egg whites

1 Cos (Romaine) lettuce heart

⅓ cup/50 g/2 oz green peas

1 spring onion (scallion), finely chopped

½ tsp ginger root, finely chopped

1 tsp salt

1 tbsp cornflour (cornstarch) mixed with 2 tbsp water

50 ml/2 fl oz milk

oil for deep-frying

1 tsp sesame seed oil

Preparation

1 Cut the bean curd into long, thin strips and blanch in a pan of salted boiling water to harden. Remove and drain.

2 Lightly beat the egg whites. Add the cornflour mixture and milk.

3 Wash and separate the lettuce heart. If you use frozen peas, make sure they are thoroughly defrosted.

4 Wait for the bean curd to cook and then coat with the egg whites, cornflour and milk mixture.

Cooking

1 Heat the oil in a wok or deep-fryer until it is very hot. Turn off the heat and let the oil cool a bit before adding the bean curd coated with the egg whites and cornflour mixture. Cook for about 1-1½ minutes and then scoop out with a slotted spoon and drain.

2 Pour off the excess oil leaving about one tablespoon in the wok. Increase the heat and stir-fry the lettuce heart with a pinch of salt. Remove and set aside on a serving dish.

3 Heat another tablespoon of oil in the wok and add the finely chopped spring onion and ginger root followed by the peas, salt and a little water. When the mixture starts to boil, add the bean curd strips. Blend well, add the sesame seed oil, and serve on the bed of lettuce heart.

SICHUAN BEAN CURD (TOFU)

2 tbsp / 10 g / ¼ oz dried wood (tree) ears (black fungus) or dried Chinese mushrooms

3 cakes bean curd (tofu)

1-2 leeks or 2-3 spring onions (scallions)

3 tbsp oil

1 tsp salted black beans

1 tbsp chilli bean paste

2 tbsp rice wine or dry sherry

1 tbsp light soy sauce

1 tsp cornflour (cornstarch) mixed with 1 tbsp cold water

Sichuan pepper, freshly ground to garnish

Preparation

1 Soak the wood ears in water for 20-25 minutes, rinse them clean, discard any hard roots and then drain. If you use dried mushrooms, they should be soaked in hot or warm water for at least 30-35 minutes. Squeeze them dry, throw out the hard stalks and cut into small pieces, retaining the water for later use.

2 Cut the bean curd into 1-cm / ½-in square cubes. Blanch them in a pan of boilng water for 2-3 minutes, remove and drain.

3 Cut the leeks or spring onions into short lengths.

Cooking

Heat the oil in a hot wok until it smokes and stir-fry the leeks or spring onions and the wood ears or mushrooms for about 1 minute. Add the salted black beans, crush them with the scooper or spatula and blend well. Now add the bean curd, the chilli bean paste, rice wine or sherry and soy sauce and continue stirring to blend. Add a little water and cook for 3-4 minutes more. Finally add the cornflour and water mixture to thicken the gravy. Serve hot with freshly ground Sichuan pepper as garnish.

BRAISED AUBERGINES (EGGPLANT)

275 g / 10 oz aubergines (eggplant)
2½ cups / 600 ml / 1 pt oil for deep-frying
2 tbsp soy sauce
1 tbsp sugar
2 tbsp water
1 tsp sesame seed oil

Preparation

Choose the long, purple variety of aubergine, rather than the large round kind if possible. Discard the stalks and cut the aubergines into diamond-shaped chunks.

Cooking

1 Heat oil in a wok until hot. Deep-fry the aubergine chunks in batches until golden. Remove with a slotted spoon and drain.

2 Pour off excess oil leaving about 1 tbsp in the wok. Return the aubergines to the wok and add the soy sauce, sugar and water. Cook over a fairly high heat for about 2 minutes, adding more water if necessary. Stir occasionally. When the juice is reduced to almost nothing, add the sesame seed oil, blend well and serve.

'THREE WHITES' IN CREAM SAUCE

275 g / 10 oz Chinese cabbage hearts
275 g / 10 oz canned white asparagus spears
1-2 celery hearts
1 tbsp oil
1 spring onion (scallion), cut into short lengths
2-3 slices ginger root, peeled
1½ tsp salt
1 tsp sugar
125 ml / 4 fl oz milk
1 tbsp cornflour (cornstarch) mixed with 3 tbsp cold water

Preparation and Cooking

1 Cut the cabbage hearts lengthwise into thin strips. Blanch them in boiling water until they are soft and remove and arrange them neatly in the middle of a long serving dish.

2 Drain and place the asparagus spears on one side of the cabbage hearts.

3 Cut the celery hearts lengthwise into strips, blanch until soft and place them on the other side of the cabbage.

4 Heat the oil over low heat and add the spring onions and ginger root to flavour the oil. Discard as soon as they start turning brown. Add the milk, salt and sugar and bring to the boil. Add the cornflour and water mixture to thicken, stir to make it smooth and pour evenly over the vegetables. Serve hot or cold.

SAN SHIAN — 'THE THREE DELICACIES'

The Chinese like to combine a number of different ingredients in a harmonious balance of colour, texture and flavour and then give the dish a poetic descriptive name, such as **Four Treasures, Two Winters** or **Three Delicacies**. They are also superstitious and consider certain numbers lucky, particularly two, three, four, five and eight.

250 g/9 oz winter bamboo shoots

100 g/4 oz oyster or straw mushrooms

275 g/10 oz fried gluten or deep-fried bean curd (tofu)

4 tbsp oil

1½ tsp salt

1 tsp sugar

1 tbsp light soy sauce

1 tsp sesame seed oil

fresh coriander leaves to garnish (optional)

Preparation

1 Cut the bamboo shoots into thin slices. The oyster mushrooms can be left whole if small; otherwise halve of quarter them. Straw mushrooms can be left whole.

2 See my remarks for Fried Gluten on page 95.

Cooking

1 Heat the oil in a hot wok or frying-pan, swirling it so that most of the surface is well greased. When the oil starts to smoke, add the bamboo shoots and mushrooms and stir-fry for about 1 minute. Add the gluten or bean curd together with salt, sugar and soy sauce. Continue stirring for 1-1½ minutes longer adding a little water if necessary. Finally add the sesame seed oil, blend well and serve hot.

2 This dish can also be served cold. In that case, you might like to separate the three main ingredients, arrange them in three neat rows and garnish with fresh coriander leaves.

BRAISED 'THREE PRECIOUS JEWELS'

2 cakes of bean curd (tofu)

225 g/8 oz broccoli or mange-tout (snow peas)

225 g/8 oz carrots

4 tbsp oil

1 tsp salt

1 tsp sugar

1 tbsp light soy sauce

1 tbsp rice wine or dry sherry

Preparation

1 Cut the bean curd into small pieces.

2 Cut the broccoli into florets. Peel the stems and cut diagonally into small pieces.

3 Peel the carrots and cut diagonally into small chunks.

Cooking

1 Heat about half of the oil in a hot wok or frying-pan. Add the bean curd pieces and shallow-fry on both sides until golden. Remove and keep aside.

2 Heat the rest of the oil. When very hot, stir-fry the broccoli and carrots for about 1-1½ minutes. Add the bean curd, salt, sugar, wine and soy sauce and continue stirring, adding a little water if necessary. Cook for 2-3 minutes if you like the broccoli and carrots to be crunchy. If not, cook another minute or two. This dish is best served hot.

VEGETARIAN 'LION'S HEAD' CASSEROLE

'Lion's head' in Chinese cuisine means pork meatballs with cabbage. Here the 'meatballs' are entirely made from vegetables.

- 4 cakes of bean curd (tofu)
- 100 g / 4 oz fried gluten
- 50 g / 2 oz cooked carrots
- 4-5 dried Chinese mushrooms, soaked
- 50 g / 2 oz bamboo shoots
- 6 cabbage or lettuce hearts
- 5 large cabbage leaves
- 1 tsp finely chopped ginger root
- 2 tbsp rice wine or dry sherry
- 1 tbsp salt
- 1 tsp sugar
- 1 tsp white pepper (ground)
- 2 tsp sesame seed oil
- 1 tbsp cornflour (cornstarch)
- 2-3 tbsp / 25 g / 1 oz ground rice or breadcrumbs
- oil for deep-frying
- Plain (all-purpose) flour for dusting

Preparation

1 Squeeze as much liquid as possible from the bean curd using cheese cloth or muslin and then mash.

2 Finely chop the gluten, carrots, mushrooms and bamboo shoots. Place them with the mashed bean curd in a large mixing bowl. Add 1 teaspoon salt, the finely chopped ginger root, ground rice, cornflour and sesame seed oil and blend everything together until smooth. Make 10 'meatballs' from this mixture and place them on a plate lightly dusted with flour.

3 Trim off any hard or tough roots from the cabbage or lettuce hearts.

Cooking

1 Heat the oil in a wok or deep-fryer. When hot, deep-fry the 'meatballs' for about 3 minutes stirring very gently to make sure that they are not stuck together. Scoop out with a slotted spoon or strainer and drain.

2 Pour off the excess oil leaving about 2 tablespoons in the wok. Stir-fry the cabbage hearts with a little salt and sugar. Add about 2½ cups / 600 ml / 1 pt water and bring to the boil. Reduce the heat and let the mixture simmer.

3 Meanwhile, line the bottom of a casserole with the cabbage leaves and place the 'meatballs' on top. Pour the cabbage hearts with the soup into the casserole and add the remaining salt, ground pepper and rice wine. Cover, bring to the boil, reduce the heat and simmer for 10 minutes.

4 To serve, take off the lid and rearrange the cabbage hearts so that they appear between the 'meatballs' in a star-shaped pattern.

SHANGHAI VEGETABLE CASSEROLE

For some reason, the best vegetarian restaurants in China are found in Shanghai — a thriving commercial centre and seaport which had a very racy reputation in the past. Most of their dishes are too complicated for the ordinary housewife or untrained layman to make, but here I have adapted a recipe which is truly simple and yet delicious.

- 6-8 dried Chinese mushrooms
- 2 cakes bean curd (tofu) or 50 g / 2 oz deep-fried bean curd
- 175 g / 6 oz broccoli
- 175 g / 6 oz bamboo shoots or carrots
- 4-5 tbsp oil
- 1½ tsp salt
- 1 tsp sugar
- 1 tbsp light soy sauce
- 2 tbsp rice wine or dry sherry
- 1 tsp cornflour (cornstarch) mixed with 1 tbsp cold water
- 1 tsp sesame seed oil

Preparation

1 Soak the dried mushrooms in warm water for 25-30 minutes, squeeze dry, discard the hard stalks and cut into thin slices. Retain the mushroom water.

2 Cut each cake of bean curd into about 12 pieces, deep-fry until golden and put to one side.

3 Cut the broccoli and bamboo shoots or carrots into diamond-shaped chunks.

Cooking

1 Heat the oil in a flameproof casserole or saucepan and stir-fry the broccoli and bamboo shoots or carrots for about 2 minutes. Add the mushrooms, bean curd, salt, sugar, soy sauce, wine and the liquid in which the mushrooms were soaked. Stir and bring the mixture to the boil. Cover and simmer over low heat for 10-15 minutes.

2 Increase the heat to high, and add the cornflour and water mixture to thicken the gravy. Cook uncovered for a minute or two. Add the sesame seed oil and serve hot.

BRAISED SPRING GREEN (COLLARD) HEARTS

Ideally, use the hearts from the spring greens (collards) after the outer leaves have been removed for the Crispy 'seaweed' recipe (page 36). Otherwise, select small ones from an oriental food store.

- 400-450 g / ¾-1 lb spring green (collard) hearts
- 3-4 tbsp oil
- 1 tsp salt
- 1 tsp sugar
- 1 tbsp light soy sauce

Preparation

There is very little preparation. Just trim off the hard and tough roots if any.

Cooking

1 Parboil the spring greens in a pot of boiling water for about 1 minute and then rinse them in cold water to preserve their bright green colour.

2 Heat the oil in a hot wok or frying-pan and stir-fry the greens with salt and sugar. Cook for about 1-1½ minutes. Add the soy sauce and a little water and braise for another minute at the most. Serve hot.

STRINGLESS (GREEN) BEANS IN GARLIC SAUCE

400 g/14 oz stringless (green) beans
1 large or 2 small cloves of garlic
3 tbsp oil
1 tsp salt
1 tsp sugar
1 tbsp light soy sauce

Preparation

1 Trim the beans. Leave them whole if they are young and tender; otherwise, cut them in half.

2 Crush and finely chop the garlic.

Cooking

1 Blanch the beans in a pan of lightly salted boiling water, drain and plunge in cold water to stop the cooking and to preserve the beans' bright green colour.

2 Heat the oil in a hot wok or frying-pan. When it starts to smoke, add the crushed garlic to flavour the oil. Before the colour of the garlic turns dark brown, add the beans and stir-fry for about 1 minute. Add the salt, sugar and soy sauce and continue stirring for another minute at most. Serve hot or cold.

RICE, NOODLES & SWEETS

Rice and noodles provide the bulk in the Chinese meal. Most of these recipes though can be served on their own as a light meal or snack. In China, noodles are always served at birthday celebrations, the length of the noodles being considered to represent long life. Spring rolls can be served as an appetizer or part of a buffet.
The Chinese do not normally conclude with a dessert, but as a compromise, I have included three for those who are used to finishing off a meal with something sweet.

Almond junket

BOILED RICE

The best plain boiled rice is obtained by using only the long grain rice known as patna. Should you prefer your rice to be softer and less fluffy, use half long grain rice and half rounded, pudding rice and reduce the amount of water for cooking by a quarter.

1¼ cups / 275 g / 10 oz long grain rice

2½ cups / 600 ml / 1 pt water

Preparation

Wash and rinse the rice in cold water until clean.

Cooking

Bring the water to the boil in a saucepan over high heat. Add the washed rice and bring back to the boil. Stir the rice with a spoon to prevent it sticking to the bottom of the pan and then cover the pan tightly with a lid and reduce the heat to very low. Cook gently for 15-20 minutes.

Note It is best not to serve the rice immediately. Fluff it up with a fork or spoon and leave it under cover in the pan for 10 minutes or so before serving.

EGG-FRIED RICE

To use up leftover cooked rice, fry it with eggs. If you add a little finely chopped spring onion (scallions) and/or green peas, you will improve not only its flavour but its appearance as well.

- 3 eggs
- 2 spring onions (scallions), finely chopped
- 1 tsp salt
- 4 tbsp oil
- ⅔ cup / 100 g / 4 oz green peas
- 4 cups / 600 g / 20 oz cooked rice
- 1 tbsp light soy sauce (optional)

Preparation

Lightly beat the eggs with about half of the finely chopped spring onions and a pinch of salt.

Cooking

1 Heat about half of the oil in a hot wok or frying-pan, pour in the beaten eggs and lightly scramble until set. Remove.

2 Heat the remaining oil and when hot, add the remaining spring onions followed by the green peas and stir-fry for about 30 seconds. Add the cooked rice and stir to separate each grain. Add the salt and soy sauce together with the eggs and stir to break the eggs into small pieces. Serve as soon as everything is well blended.

VEGETARIAN SPECIAL FRIED RICE

Vegetarian special fried rice is one stage richer and more elaborate than egg-fried rice and almost a meal in itself.

- 4-6 dried Chinese mushrooms
- 1 green pepper, cored and seeded
- 1 red pepper, cored and seeded
- 100 g / 4 oz bamboo shoots
- 2 eggs
- 2 spring onions (scallions), finely chopped
- 2 tsp salt
- 4-5 tbsp oil
- 6 cups / 900 g / 30 oz cooked rice
- 1 tbsp light soy sauce (optional)

Preparation

1 Soak the dried mushrooms in warm water for 25-30 minutes, squeeze dry and discard the hard stalks. Cut the mushrooms into small cubes.

2 Cut the green and red peppers and the bamboo shoots into small cubes.

3 Lightly beat the eggs with about half of the spring onions and a pinch of the salt.

Cooking

1 Heat about 2 tablespoons of oil in a hot wok, add the beaten eggs and scramble until set. Remove.

2 Heat the remaining oil. When hot, add the rest of the spring onions followed by all the vegetables and stir-fry until each piece is covered with oil. Add the cooked rice and salt and stir to separate each grain of rice. Finally add the soy sauce, blend everything together and serve.

CHOW MEIN — FRIED NOODLES

After **chop suey, chow mein** (which means 'fried noodles' in Chinese) must be the next most popular dish in Chinese restaurants. Try to get freshly made noodles from an Oriental food store or Italian delicatessen, as they taste much better than dried ones. As a rough guide, allow at least 50 g/2 oz dried noodles per person, and double the weight if using freshly made ones.

25 g/1 oz dried bean curd skin sticks
⅔ cup/25 g/1 oz dried tiger lily buds
50 g/2 oz bamboo shoots
100 g/4 oz spinach or any other greens
225 g/8 oz dried egg noodles
2 spring onions (scallions), thinly shredded
3-4 tbsp oil
1 tsp salt
2 tbsp light soy sauce
2 tsp sesame seed oil

Preparation

1 Soak the dried vegetables overnight in cold water or in hot water for at least an hour. When soft, thinly shred both the bean curd skins and tiger lily buds.

2 Shred the bamboo shoots and spinach leaves into thin strips.

Cooking

1 Cook the noodles in a pan of boiling water according to the instructions on the packet. Depending on the thickness of the noodles, this should take 5 minutes or so. Freshly made noodles will take only about half that time.

2 Heat about half the oil in a hot wok or frying-pan. While waiting for it to smoke, drain the noodles in a sieve. Add them with about half the spring onions and the soy sauce to the wok and stir-fry. Do not overcook, or the noodles will become soggy. Remove and place them on a serving dish.

3 Add the rest of the oil to the wok. When hot, add the other spring onions and stir a few times. Then add all the vegetables and continue stirring. After 30 seconds or so, add the salt and the remaining soy sauce together with a little water if necessary. As soon as the gravy starts to boil, add the sesame seed oil and blend everything well. Place the mixture on top of the fried noodles as a dressing.

Note Of course you can use substitutes for any of the ingredients in the dressing. For instance, instead of dried bean curd skin, you can use dried Chinese mushrooms or fresh mushrooms. Instead of tiger lily buds, why not use fresh bean sprouts or shredded celery, carrots, green peppers, cucumber, cabbage, lettuce or onions and so on. It is contrast of texture and colour that is important.

VEGETARIAN NOODLES IN SOUP

See my general remarks on choosing and cooking noodles for chow mein (page 119).

225 g/8 oz water chestnuts
100 g/4 oz straw mushrooms
100 g/4 oz white nuts
3 tbsp oil
1 tsp salt
1 tsp sugar
1 tbsp light soy sauce
1 tsp sesame seed oil
225 g/8 oz egg noodles or vermicelli

Preparation

Very little preparation is required. Drain the ingredients if they are canned and cut the water chestnuts into thin slices. The straw mushrooms and white nuts can be left whole.

Cooking

1 Heat the oil in a hot wok or frying-pan. When it starts to smoke, add the vegetables and stir-fry for a few seconds. Add the salt, sugar and soy sauce and continue stirring. When the gravy begins to boil, reduce the heat and let it simmer gently.

2 Cook the noodles in boiling water (see the recipe on page 119). Drain and place them in a large serving bowl. Pour a little of the water in which the noodles were cooked into the bowl — just enough to half-cover the noodles. Then quickly pour the entire contents of the wok or frying-pan over the top. Garnish with the sesame seed oil and serve hot.

Note The seasoning can be adjusted. For instance, freshly ground pepper or chilli sauce can be added to give the dish a lift.

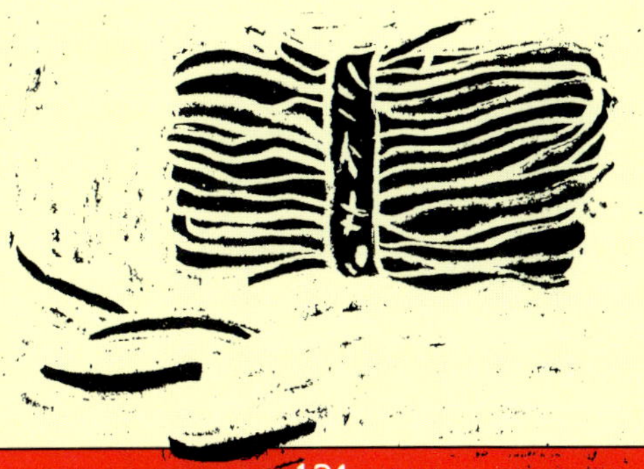

VEGETARIAN SPRING ROLLS

1 pack of 20 frozen spring roll skins
225 g/8 oz fresh bean sprouts
225 g/8 oz young tender leeks or spring onions (scallions)
100 g/4 oz carrots
100 g/4 oz white mushrooms
oil for deep-frying
1½ tsp salt
1 tsp sugar
1 tbsp light soy sauce

Preparation

1 Take the spring roll skins out of the packet and leave them to defrost thoroughly under a damp cloth.

2 Wash and rinse the bean sprouts in a bowl of cold water and discard the husks and other bits and pieces that float to the surface. Drain.

3 Cut the leeks or spring onions, carrots and mushrooms into thin shreds.

Cooking the filling

Heat 3-4 tablespoons of oil in a preheated wok or frying pan and stir-fry all the vegetables for a few seconds. Add the salt, sugar and soy sauce and continue stirring for about 1-1½ minutes. Remove and leave to cool a little.

Cooking the spring rolls

Heat about 6⅓ cups/1.5 L/2½ pt oil in a wok or deep fryer until it smokes. Reduce the heat or even turn it off for a few minutes to cool the oil a little before adding the spring rolls. Deep-fry 6-8 at a time for 3-4 minutes or until golden and crispy. Increase the heat to high again before frying each batch. As each batch is cooked, remove and drain it on absorbent paper. Serve hot with a dip sauce such as soy sauce, vinegar, chilli sauce or mustard.

Note These spring rolls are ideal for a buffet-style meal or as cocktail snacks.

VEGETARIAN SPRING ROLLS

Left Cut each spring roll skin in half diagonally

Right Place about two teaspoons of the filling on the skin about a third of the way down, with the triangle pointing away from you.

Left, right Lift the lower flap over the filling and roll once.

Left, right Fold in both ends and roll once more.

Left, right Brush the upper edge with a little flour and water paste and roll into a neat package. Repeat until all the filling is used up. These can be kept in the refrigerator for a couple of days or frozen for up to 3 months.

RED BEAN PASTE PANCAKES

2 cups / 225 g / 8 oz plain (all-purpose) flour
125 ml / 4 fl oz boiling water
1 egg
3 tbsp oil
4-5 tbsp / 100 g / 4 oz sweetened red bean paste or chestnut purée

Preparation

1 Sift the flour into a mixing bowl and very gently pour in the boiling water. Add about 1 teaspoon oil and the beaten egg.

2 Knead the mixture into a firm dough and then divide it into 2 equal portions. Roll out each portion into a long 'sausage' on a lightly floured surface and cut it into 4-6 pieces. Using the palm of your hand, press each piece into a flat pancake.

3 On a lightly floured surface, flatten each pancake into a 15-cm / 6-in circle with a rolling pin and roll gently.

Cooking

1 Place an ungreased frying-pan on a high heat. When hot, reduce the heat to low and place one pancake at a time in the pan. Turn it over when little brown spots appear on the underside. Remove and keep under a damp cloth until you have finished making all the pancakes.

2 Spread about 2 tablespoons red bean paste or chestnut purée over about 80% of the pancake surface and roll it over three or four times to form a flattened roll.

3 Heat the oil in a frying-pan and shallow-fry the pancakes until golden brown, turning over once.

4 Cut each pancake into 3-4 pieces and serve hot or cold.

RED BEAN PASTE PANCAKES

TOFFEE BANANAS

- 4 bananas, peeled
- 1 egg
- 2 tbsp plain (all-purpose) flour
- oil for deep-frying
- 4 tbsp sugar
- 1 tbsp cold water

Preparation

1 Cut the bananas in half lengthwise and then cut each half into two crosswise.

2 Beat the egg, add the flour and mix well to make a smooth batter.

Cooking

1 Heat the oil in a wok or deep-fryer. Coat each piece of banana with batter and deep fry until golden. Remove and drain.

2 Pour off the excess oil leaving about 1 tablespoon of oil in the wok. Add the sugar and water and stir over a medium heat to dissolve the sugar. Continue stirring and when the sugar has caramelized, add the hotbanana pieces. Coat well and remove. Dip the hot bananas in cold water to harden the toffee and serve immediately.

Toffee bananas *(opposite,*

ALMOND JUNKET

This junket can be made from **agar-agar**, isinglass or gelatine. When chilled and served with a variety of fresh and canned fruit, it is a most refreshing dessert.

- 10 g / ⅓ oz agar-agar or isinglass (or 25 g / 1 oz gelatine powder)
- 4 tbsp sugar
- 5 oz / 150 ml / ¼ pt evaporated milk
- 10 oz / 600 ml / 1 pt water
- 1 tsp almond essence (extract)
- 1 can cherries or mixed fruit salad with syrup to garnish

Preparation

Dissolve the agar-agar or isinglass and the sugar with water in two separate pans over gentle heat. (If using gelatine powder, just follow the instructions on the packets.) Add milk and almond essence and pour the mixture into a large serving bowl. Allow to cool for at least 30 minutes and then place in the refrigerator for 2-3 hours to set. To serve, cut the junket into small cubes and pour the canned fruit and syrup over it.

INDEX